NOT WITHOUT OUR WITHOUT CHILDREN

UNVEILING THE HIDDEN JEWELS OF PARENTING

KATHLEEN MUNGAL

Produced by:

FriesenPress
Suite 300 – 852 Fort Street
Victoria, BC, Canada V8W 1H8

www.friesenpress.com

Distributed to the trade by The Ingram Book Company

TABLE OF CONTENTS

This book is dedicated to my husband who has demonstrated that love can be beautiful, exciting and fulfilling. It is only by his encouragement and belief in me that this book was completed. Also to our children; Karleen, Kristan & Jose, Kanesha, Kyra, Jadon, Jayonna and Janelle, who are truly gifts from the Lord.

"Pour out your heart like water
before the face of the Lord.
Lift your hands toward Him for the
life of your young children."
LAMENTATIONS 2:19

Kathleen lives in Bolton, Ontario and is a proud mother of seven beautiful children, (one married daughter). She has been married since 1990 to her husband Harrison. She shares the quality of a mother's heart touching many lives around the world. She has a passion to support mothers to be effective in raising their children. Kathleen teaches on the role of a woman and the need to keep their identity. She believes that her greatest strength is her example.

Kathleen has been a guest speaker at schools, churches, workshops, seminars, conferences etc. sharing alongside with her husband on relationships, parenting, womanhood and other related topics revolving around marriage and the family. Kathleen has been the keynote speaker to many international women seminars in Paris- France, Lima- Peru, Santa Clara-Cuba, Split-Croatia, Canada, USA and other countries.

Kathleen has taught for over 12 years at Bible Colleges on a variety of courses and co-pastored with her husband at 4 different churches, including being a missionary for 2 years in Croatia. She is currently involved with her husband in a leadership role at her local church, along with their senior pastors.

Kathleen holds a diploma in Developmentally Service Worker (DSW). She is ordained with and a member of Open Bible Faith Fellowship Canada. Kathleen has been awarded on several occasions for her community work particularly through Age to Age Training, Education and Counselling Inc.

FOREWORD

It has been my privilege to watch Kathleen walk through many seasons of parenthood - taking care of babies, toddlers, children, teens, and now as her oldest are stepping out of the home into life's adventure of beginning their own families and careers. This is not a book of theory but practical life experience. God's plan has always been for your family to be blessed.

If you want a godly family, read this book and then apply the principles to your family. They will work for you! You will want to share these godly principles and life stories with others. With tools like this we can change society – one family at a time.

Pastor Jill Neilson
Co-Pastor
Bramalea Christian Fellowship

INTRODUCTION

My husband approached me one day with an idea for a book he was thinking of writing. As soon as he told me the title "Not without our children", I was hooked. It brought me back several years ago, before we started our bible school, to the day my husband said, "I think the bible school we will start should be tuition-free." I knew right there and then that it was a "God idea". What do I mean by this? I mean that this was not just something my husband thought up; it got a hold of me and the Spirit of God within me whispered "yes, that's it".

The Holy Spirit is still saying, "Yes, that's it" as the bible school has expanded and lives have been touched. Students who normally could not afford bible school have attended and have been trained in the Word and in practice. God has called each of us individually to step out in the call and vision He has set before us. My husband and I rejoice each time we see a student step out and touch lives for the glory of His name.

Doors have opened in the last while to include ministering to couples through clinical counselling (www.agetoage.ca) and seminars, "Kissing Break-ups Goodbye" being the most recent venture. Through counselling sessions and seminars, we have been helping couples understand each other's needs and equipping them with the necessary skills and knowledge to create healthy relationships.

Our pastors have been greatly instrumental in encouraging and mentoring us to be able to push forward in ministry. They have a passion to see the church family as well as the community reach their full potential in their relationships - advancing and enlarging the kingdom for more to belong!

But as we train and do the Lord's work we must protect and nurture the very gift God has given us to support and love us and, that is the family. Too many ministries have been destroyed because the family unit is put on the back burner. Many pursue ministry at all cost…. but at the expense of the family. I can picture our heavenly Father shaking his head in sorrow at the hurt and shame we put upon each other. What makes it more shameful is that we put it under "the price" of the ministry and keep going on, not dealing with the real issue.

Having a large family of our own, we know the struggles and difficulties associated with balancing a home and a ministry or two. Add a job as well and you have quite a package to deal with. The key is to know your priorities and set your boundaries - something we will deal with later in this book.

I pray as you read this book you will have a clearer understanding of how family and ministry work. My husband and I am by no means the perfect model but through our experiences and our study of the Word we pray that you will have the same desire we have. That is, the desire to see our families work together in the ministry, first as family members and secondly as co-workers for Christ. Be blessed today!

1 FOUNDATIONS FIRST

I want to begin this book by sharing what's been on my heart for the last few years. Through my observation I have seen that many people today spend too much of their time running from place to place, trying this out and trying out that. They are telling themselves that if an opportunity looks good they must have it or, if a ministry someone else is involved in looks goods, they should be a part of it. They tell themselves that their family will understand. Why shouldn't they? It is work that is being done for the Lord. So what if I am not home that often? My family should understand; it's ministry and ministry comes first. You would be surprised to know how many people involved in ministry think this way. No foundation is being laid in the family or even the ministry. Our eyes follow what looks good and because it is ministry, in our own mind we decide it has to be the right choice.

The family unit is being battered and pushed aside, all for the sake of ministry. We need to take a long look at some facts and consider what is important. I want to share some foundational principles that will help balance these two important facets of our life, ministry and the family.

In order to begin a project or even attempt to start a ministry we must look at building a foundation. A foundation is what holds up any building, home or structure and supports it. If your foundation is not strong - or, has been built poorly - and was rushed to be completed, it will not sustain the weight put upon it. It can begin to crack, shaking the building built upon it, disturbing it and its contents, and creating havoc and destruction. All the work you put into the finished product is now destroyed in a short time and all because the foundation was not strong.

Jesus shares with us a parable of the wise and foolish builders. In Matthew 7:24-27 Jesus says, *"Therefore, whoever hears these saying of Mine, and does them, I will liken him to a wise man who built his house on the rock; and the rain descended, the floods came, and the winds blew and beat on that house; and it did not fall, for it was founded on the rock. But everyone who hears these sayings of Mine, and does not do them will be like a foolish man who built his house on the sand: and the rain descended, the floods came, and the winds blew and beat on that house; and it fell. And great was its fall."*

This parable shows us the absolute necessity of building a strong foundation. Doing the will of God and hearing His voice create an opportunity to build firmly and correctly. If we do not concern ourselves with creating a good foundation we will pay for it later and all our work will be in vain.

You may ask, "How does this relate to the family and ministry?" This is what I want you to think about. How does building a foundation relate to you, and your desire to fulfil your call in the ministry?

Let's start from the beginning. The book of Genesis tells us in chapter 1:27, "*so God created man in His own image; in the image of God He created him; male and female He created them.*" This is a wonderful verse describing the family order. In the previous verse God said, "*Let us make man in Our image, according to Our likeness...*" *vs 26a.*

Many scholars interpret this as a reference to the Trinity. That is, One God and yet a community of persons. Then God creates man in His own image. He creates man as male and female not one person but two people. Yet, as we read on in Genesis 2:24 the two individuals when joined together become one flesh. "*Therefore a man shall leave his father and mother and be joined to his wife and they shall become one flesh.*"

Who reflects God's image? God chose to create man and woman in His own image and through this union he created marriage, a family. So when you think about the community of the family it is a reflection of the community in the Godhead. The identity we have as a family, the life that sustains and the power that comes from the unity of the family all comes from God, a reflection of His Image. Isn't that powerful! Already in the beginning of creation God had a plan for the family. God originally set the foundation for us to build our marriage on. The Bible tells us that, "*Unless the Lord builds the house, they labour in vain who build it.*" Psalm 127:1

God placed dreams and visions in our hearts and there is a reason for that. God created us in His Image and therefore has instilled in us the same dreams and visions that He would have for the future. We need to have a vision for the family. We need to see our family past today and into the future. We need to see the family as God sees it, full of potential and promise.

When we think about vision we can look at it like a blueprint, spread out before us. Each family has its own unique blueprint specifically modified for them. Some details and plans are open for change and modification but others are definitely not! Blueprints are plans that take time to draw up; success comes from collaboration and commitment to the plan. Blueprints are vital to building the foundation and plan of the family. Proverbs 29:18 says, "Where there is no vision, the people perish." A vision sets the foundation for the family and the standard for future generations.

THE ARCHITECT

Once the blueprint is laid out, the vision written down and spoken over the family unit then the building program can begin. Who is the one that now draws up the plan? It is the Architect, the master planner, he works with the vision and plans out the building project; that is none other than the Father Himself. He sets the vision in our hearts, the desire to build, and works with us to see it come to pass. If our vision for the family does not come from His heart it is set for failure. We must at all times check our vision with the will of the Father. Is it a godly vision? Does it glorify God and witness to others? Does it include all the members of the house, working together for a common goal?

Raising seven children in today's society is no easy feat but when you include each and every member of the family in the planning of your future, allowing them to impart their gifts and talents towards the vision or common goal then something beautiful takes place. You now have a whole army at your disposal, working side by side and watching each other's back.

My husband recently began a new tradition with our family. At the beginning of the year we sit down around the supper table with all our children and start to discuss what we would like to accomplish for the year. We go around the table from the youngest to the oldest, each sharing five of their goals for the year. Following the discussion, each family member is asked to write these five goals down and put it in a sealed envelope. At the end of the year we would sit down together and open the envelopes and thank the Lord for what He has accomplished through each one of us in that year.

I see this practice as working the vision of the family. Each of us is partaking and contributing toward the good of the family and toward glorifying the Lord. If we do not include our children in the vision of the family then the vision has no effect. We will be a poor witness and steward of the gems that God has entrusted to us. I want to raise up a generation that will carry the vision. If we do not raise up future vision carriers then the vision will die with us.

THE BUILDER

Now that we have an Architect, we need to find a builder to be in charge of the project. Who has the ability to carry out the Architect's plans correctly and with a spirit of excellence? Who has the authority to build in our lives and carry on the work of the Architect on a more personal level? A builder is someone with whom you deal directly and develop a relationship on a personal level. The builder is in charge of the project and it is His building and His name goes on it. The builder is Jesus Christ. His name should be stamped all over our hearts and family as the master builder. Is He the builder of your family unit? We need to ask ourselves these questions so we certain who is in charge. People need to see Jesus not only in us as individuals but as a family.

I think the greatest witness we have as a family serving the Lord is the outer witness to our community. We live in a smaller community outside the city and we love the fact that people recognize you, know your name, and actually take time to ask how you are doing. I have started to see the impact our family can have as people watch our family dynamics in action around the community. My children are examples to their teachers, their friends and the people on their paper route or employers in the community. When I go into the library, the bank and the local stores I constantly receive comments on our family and the example they are setting. This then gives me the opportunity to share the reason why they can be examples and that is Jesus, our Saviour. The community is watching us and we are walking examples whether we like it or not. If people are not seeing Jesus in our family, but only discord and complacency then we are failing in our call.

The builder lays the foundations, the cornerstones of the home. I recently noticed a beautiful house in our neighbourhood. The house is very well kept with a meticulously groomed front yard and well placed ornaments throughout the front area. Front and centre is a large gemlike stone engraved with the house number. I asked around and found out that this is the builder's home, the builder who built most of the homes in the neighbourhood. His mark was on the home and property; his reputation and business depend on the quality of work he produces and projects. Do we allow the builder of our family to mark us as a product of His hands? Will people look at us and understand who the builder of our family unit is? Jesus is our chief cornerstone, the builder and foundation of our lives and our homes. He should receive the glory for the marvellous workmanship He implements in our homes.

He never stops the building project or puts it on hold. We may do that by ourselves, in an attempt to change or slow down the building process. We want to make changes that fit our individual needs instead of the needs of the family. Jesus, however, sees the bigger picture and knows exactly what is needed for the future and builds appropriately. We just need to trust Him at His word.

THE INSPECTOR

The building is now being built, the builder's name is on the project and the walls are going up. But as we build who is going to check that we are doing a good job? Are we building those walls properly and to the right standard? There is one person who can help us. He sees errors and encourages excellence. He gently urges us to correct our mistakes and pushes us toward a more excellent way. He is the Inspector - the Holy Spirit. He lets us know when we need to be on guard against the attacks of the enemy. There are so many areas of attack that come against the family unit. We can see critics speaking against us and the way we raise our children. Members of the family can struggle with unfaithfulness, selfishness, fear, rebellion and divorce. All these are attacks against our building program and the Holy Spirit is the one who leads and guides us, drawing us closer to Him and further away from the attacks.

Many people think that when you raise your children in the ways of the Lord you will be free from the attacks of the enemy but this is untrue. When you have set a high moral standard for your children be sure that it will be tested at times. One thing I have learned to accept is that my children will behave like children at times; they are not adults and that they will make mistakes or make poor decisions. This is a process of growth for them that they must go through. It is what we do with our mistakes and how we learn from them that shape us to be future leaders. There are many past spiritual leaders whom I have studied that have made bad decisions and mistakes but it was those who learned from them and persevered that made the biggest impact on society in the past as well as today.

One example of this is a person by the name of Kathryn Kuhlman. She was really starting to expand her evangelistic meetings and even settled down by opening her own church called "Denver Revival Tabernacle". This church had about two thousand seats and was a site for nightly meetings every day, except Mondays, for four years. It was during this time that she met a handsome evangelist named Burroughs A. Waltrip. He was married and had two children, but shortly after meeting Kathryn he divorced his wife and told everyone that his wife had left him. Kathryn became romantically involved with him despite all the warnings issued by her friends and co-workers. She reasoned that his wife left him making him free to marry. They were secretly married. Even before the marriage Kathryn confessed to her friends that she just couldn't seem to find the will of God in this, but because of her love for him she allowed her feelings to rule her heart.

Kathryn lost her church, her close friends and her ministry. Even her relationship with God suffered because she put her desires before God. Consequently, for the next eight years Kathryn's ministry stopped. She tried to make her marriage work but the foundation on which it was built comprised of lies and deceit and we know that this is not a strong foundation but a weak one which will eventually crumble. Her husband's ministry began to crumble as well and over the years it completely dissolved. Kathryn was a human being with temptations the same as many of us face today but what made her a great woman of God was her choice and action to recover from her mistake.

Kathryn left Waltrip and was totally restored in her life with God. She had to work hard to pick up the pieces of her ministry but eventually she finally reached the pinnacle of her ministry when healing began to take place in her ministry. The rest of her life is history as God used this mighty woman in a great healing ministry and manifestation of the Holy Spirit.

THE LABOURERS

The last group of people needed in fulfilling our vision for the family is the labourers. The labourers are the people who work the vision; they put their hands together and complete the building project, the vision. Without the labourers the vision could not be fulfilled. The labourers are you and I, working together, using our gifts and talents to see the vision carried out and fulfilled. It takes all of us, each with unique abilities and purpose. I believe that is why God has made each and every one of us so unique. We complement one another when we learn to work together, especially in the family unit.

My husband and I use our differences to build instead of tear us apart. If we learn to appreciate our differences instead of resent them we will accomplish what God had planned from the very beginning. Our differences make us unique and equip us to each carry out a different part of the plan. If we were both the same in abilities not as much would be accomplished. Too many marriages today are broken because the two parties feel they are two different people and do not appreciate one another. Meanwhile it was usually their differences that drew them together in the first place!

The vision sets forth the foundation of our families. The walls we construct, the paths that we pave, the designs we formulate will be a pattern we set for future generations. When we are gone what will remain from our efforts? Our children of course! We set the pattern for them and their children and their children's children. Family is an important part of our culture and one of our few links with the future. Society today would like to lay the foundations for us and control our destiny through our children. They are just waiting at our doorstep eager to take control over our choices and lifestyle. They want us to believe that they know what is best for our children and our future as a family. Sometimes it looks so much easier to give in to society's demands and we give up the fight for our family. But every battle has a victory and our victor has never led us in a battle that He could not win.

We must fight for our family and the values instilled in us from the very foundations of creation. Each season in our lives will bring new opportunities and also new temptations. Is it an easy task? No! Is it worth the fight? Most definitely! My greatest reward is the fruit of my labour in the family. To see your children serving the Lord is the greatest joy a parent can have.

POINTS TO PONDER

- *How did God carry out His plan for the family in creation?*

- *Our vision for the family can be planted and grown in the family unit among all its members. Name some ways we can do this.*

- *How can we learn from other people's mistakes?*

- *Fight, fight, and fight always for your family. Have you had to fight recently for your loved ones?*

- *Think of 2 qualities of your spouse that is totally different from you but can be used as a positive trait for you.*

- *There is never a battle that God cannot win for us. He is undefeatable!*

2 OUR SEED

When I think about the fact that each little life that begins in the womb has already been given a purpose and a destiny I am amazed and overwhelmed. How can all this be ingrained into this tiny being and spoken over their life while yet being formed. Our God is an amazing God and worthy to be praised! The seed of life sown into the womb is destined for great things and only God knows each child's purpose. It really humbles you to think that you can play a small part in this big picture of destiny and purpose.

The gift of life is so precious and we must guard it at all cost. The devil knows that each seed has potential to affect the world and pull down spiritual strongholds. That is why the murder of our unborn children is so common place today. Many people's conscience have been seared by continual indifference to the unborn right to life. It is justified by our teachers, media and so called leaders of this day so when we start seeing it as just another issue or "our choice" we have just locked reason and compassion from our hearts and replaced it with indifference.

I remember when our third child was arriving into this world very quickly. I had arrived at the hospital and immediately was wheeled into the hospital delivery room. The doctor that attended me was very rough in his approach and his general conduct as he performed the delivery. I did not feel comfortable with him; I felt something was off and was very troubled in my spirit. My husband and I continued to pray while dealing with the spiritual clash we felt in the room. It eased up a bit and our beautiful little girl entered the world, perfectly formed, and perfectly healthy. After the delivery we were taken to our room and I found out the real reason for my discomfort and distrust of this man. This doctor, we soon discovered, also performed abortions in the same hospital.

There is a struggle going on that seeks to destroy our children even before they leave the womb. Psalm 139: 13-16 tells us why the devil seeks to destroy us in the womb. It tells us: *"For you formed my inward parts; you covered me in my mother's womb. I will praise You, for I am fearfully and wonderfully made, marvellous are your works, and that my soul knows very well. My frame was not hidden from You, when I was made in secret, and skillfully wrought in the lowest parts of the earth. Your eyes saw my substance, being yet unformed. And in Your book they all were written, the days fashioned for me, when as yet there were none of them."*

When we look at verse 16 that says, *"Your eyes saw my substance, being yet unformed"* we discover that the Hebrew word for "my substance" indicates the embryo. God sees us in the womb even though our parts are not yet completely formed. Then the verse goes on to say that in God's book they are all written and the days are fashioned for us even when they were none of them. Our life, as well as the structure and meaning of our life are all established from the beginning by God. Wow, isn't that amazing!

To know that the God of all creation personally formed each child, including you and me is amazing! We are patterned and imprinted with the hand of God Himself, each with uniqueness all our own. There is no one else quite like you. Sure, you may have similarities in character or personality but even a twin will have something about them that sets them apart. They may look identical but each was created by the Master's hand and is an individual on their own.

Our true identity and image should mirror our creator. We should be a reflection or mirror image of God Himself for He created us in His image.

Each child forming in the womb is a potential world changer, shaker and mover. The enemy knows this very well and is seeking to destroy this seed before it even enters this world. He knows the potential that seed has to make an impact and impact future generations. Satan is hard at work destroying seed after seed.

After Jesus was born, the angel of the Lord told Joseph to flee to Egypt because Herod would seek to destroy their young child. Herod ordered the death of all male children in Bethlehem and all its districts from 2 years old and under. He sought to destroy the seed that was prophesied to be the 'King of the Jews." The very seed that would bring us our salvation and the victory over death itself was threatened!

From our very first pregnancy, my husband and I would lay hands on my womb and pray for our child. We would pray for their health, their ambitions and their future relationships.

While each child was growing inside of me in leaps and bounds, remarkably forming limbs and organs, also present was the spirit of our child, ready to receive our prayers and guidance even inside the womb. Through our prayers we were birthing vision and purpose, strength and destiny for each little one. If the devil is so interested in destroying our seeds we must see them as he sees them, potential world changers. We cannot be slack concerning their care and nurture. Our diligence must begin from the moment they are conceived. It is our responsibility as parents to care for our children and prepare them even from the time they are conceived.

The seeds that we produce are vulnerable, trusting and can be naïve to the world and all it holds. We have a great responsibility to protect and instruct those seeds that have been entrusted to us. The birds of the air are circling above our seeds seeking to devour them. The soil of the earth with its pollutants and toxins are searching for ways to corrupt and poison the minds of our children. We shoulder the task of the protecting, teaching and guiding our seeds so that they will recognize danger. They will know how to combat the enemy's attacks and be equipped to fight the fight of faith. They will recognize the Holy Spirit's voice because we have taught them how to listen.

The Bible tells us in Psalm 127:3, *"Behold, children are a heritage from the Lord; the fruit of the womb is a reward."* What the Lord has formed in the womb is a reward for us as parents. As a mother of seven who is often out in the community with my children I often get asked the question, "How many children do you have anyway?" After I answer seven, I often receive the response of, "Seven? I can't even handle one!" The more I would hear this reply, the more upset I would get. I have a hard time understanding how people can complain about a blessing or a reward the Lord has given them. But I slowly began to realize that not everyone has the revelation of the treasure that God has given them. They are just ignorant of this fact and allow the cares of the world to consume them.

I realized that I was wrong for getting upset and judging them so instead I needed to answer differently. I now share often how much of a blessing my children are to those who ask and this then opens the door to share God's goodness with someone I may never had a chance to witness to before.

The seed implanted and formed by God the Creator, who formed the universe with his hands has been entrusted into our care. We have a great responsibility as parents to nurture and protect this child and instruct him or her in the ways of the Lord.

While reading the book of Jeremiah I was again reminded of this responsibility. We may be chosen to raise the next great man or woman of God who will impact their generation for God. When God called Jeremiah as a prophet He told him, *"Before I formed you in the womb I knew you; before you were born I sanctified you; I ordained you a prophet to the nations." Jeremiah 1:5*

As parents we need to nurture the call of God on our children. Our own preconceived ideas may stand in the way of the true calling God has for them, and could lead them down a different path, away from God's plan. It may be difficult at times as we have to remember that our children are given to us by God and entrusted in our care but they are God's property and eventually will need to take that step of walking in His plan for their life. We all want our children to succeed in life and prosper with a good job and security but what if God is calling them to missions or ministry which often takes lots of sacrifice and little security. It is a tough job as a parent to allow God to lead them in these future endeavours but it is our responsibility to teach our children how to listen to His voice and make sure it is God talking to them.

This leads us to our next chapter, preparation!

POINTS TO PONDER:

- *Why is the devil so hard at work to destroy our seed before it is even birthed into this world?*

- *Whose responsibility is it to nurture, instruct and prepare the seed given by God?*

- *Do we hold them the seeds entrusted to us tightly or loosely in our hands?*

3 PREPARATION

Picture a large field, a field filled with lush grass, rolling hills and mature trees. A small brook happily gurgles in the distance sending forth an image of peace and tranquility. The plan is to build a family home amidst these trees and on top of a small hill. This dream is implanted in the hearts of a young married couple, ready to begin a family and settle in a home of their own. They are anxious to begin; they have spent many years planning.

In order to begin fulfilling this dream the ground must be prepared. The ground must be cleared of any stones or trees; roots must be pulled out and the soil dug and levelled.

During the preparation this young couple decides to seek advice from another couple who had also built their own home. They ask them how to effectively clear the trees, and how to aggressively root out the stubborn tree roots and rubble from the earth. They wisely seek advice from those who have faced these obstacles and were successful in overcoming them.

They faced some difference of opinions on where the house should be situated. The young woman wanted the house to have large bay windows overlooking the stream with a deck surrounding the back. The young man persisted in the opinion that it was better to have the deck in the front so they could observe who was coming on to their property. The pros and cons of their decisions were weighed. The young man feeling the great responsibility of protecting and providing for his family considered his wife's request. The young wife with her nurturing instincts and gift of creating a peaceful and happy environment for her home also considered her husband. Both had great ideas and giftings working inside of them but in order for these gifts to work properly they had to find a way for their ideas to work together.

Preparation for the journey of marriage and raising a family is sadly lacking in our culture today. We jump eagerly into a marriage, excited and madly "in love" without preparing for this adventure. And I truly mean adventure! We busy ourselves with buying the dress, the flowers, finding the right church and banquet hall. We forget to prepare ourselves for what happens after the wedding, when real life begins and real situations arise that will test our faith and vows we took on that day.

I remember talking to a young girl who was in the process of preparing for her wedding day. As we talked I saw the stars in her eyes and her breathless anticipation of the day. She then told me, "We will live on our love", as though it would be easy, like floating on a cloud on a breathtaking spring morning. She didn't know what was in store; their future was not planned out or discussed. Preparation for what lay ahead of her was left behind for "living on love". Sadly to say, the marriage was rocky and eventually broke apart.

When I see marriages of friends and family fall apart my heart cries out. How much heartache and confusion could be avoided if only preparation was made before the marriage! My passion for marriage and the family stems from seeing the results of poorly planned marriages and weak teaching on foundations. I weep for those affected by torn apart marriages. It pushes me to speak more passionately about these foundational truths found in the Word of God. God cares about our marriages. He cares about our families.

Family is the foundation on which our country is built. If we don't take care of our families, our society will crumble and lawlessness will prevail. The prophet Jeremiah tells us, *"I will give them one heart, and one way, that they fear me forever, for the good of them, and of their children after them. Jeremiah 32:39*

A prime example is the couple I described earlier who were preparing for their marriage. They knew they would have obstacles to face in building their home. They wisely chose to seek advice from others who have experience and, who have done it before. God has surrounded us with a community of believers who have gone before us, who have wisdom and experience. What an opportunity for us to knock at their doors and pick their brains for gems of wisdom and truths!

I remember clearly an incident, or you could say a "timely encounter" with one of my older sisters when I was preparing for marriage. I dropped by her house one evening and to my surprise she just began to share with me some truths about the differences between men and women. She shared some things that are important to men so I could be aware of this as I entered my covenant of marriage. I was shocked that she spoke so freely to me about these issues, especially about sex. She probably chuckled to herself after remembering my facial expressions of part terror and part anticipation. Today I am very thankful to her for her words of wisdom and daring to drop a bomb of reality on a starry eyed bride to be.

There are amazing couples out there who are ready to invest in lives of others that are preparing for the covenant of marriage. Just think of some families that you know of that set a good example in your community and church. Look at their strengths and ask them questions; maybe they have been through some tough times. Ask them about how they got through these experiences. Experience is our greatest teacher. It is very hard to teach intervention or prevention if you have not had to use it for yourself.

Let's go back to the example of the young couple. They had some obstacles in their building plan which most of us experience in one form or another – difference of opinions. As I mentioned earlier, the young man wanted the deck in the front; he wanted the assurance that he could see if trouble was coming. He is the protector of the family; every man should have these instincts for they are God given.

The scripture tells us in I Timothy 5:8; *"But if anyone does not provide for his own especially for those of his household, he has denied the faith and is worse than an unbeliever."* A man feels responsible for the family as a provider and protector. If he fails in this he himself feels he has failed as a person. God has placed man as the head of the household just as Christ is the head of the church. It is who he is created to be at helm and we need to allow our men to lead in their God-given role as a spiritual leader in the home.

We enter into our relationships and marriages with different ideas and opinions. Most of our beliefs stem from our background - how we were raised. But they make up who you are as a person, each unique and particular to you as an individual. We can respect that and at times even admire that but when you enter a relationship there is a blending of individuals.

Marriage molds us like clay where each person complements the other. I can picture two different pieces of clay, each with its own unique color and texture, beautiful in its own way. Now the Potter decides that these two pieces will be more effective or useful as one piece, maybe an intricate and beautifully illustrated vase or a strong and sturdy pouring pitcher. These pieces must be moulded together, each unique with its own special qualities yet when put together creates something beautiful and purposeful. Most importantly, the final product becomes an instrument that glorifies our Lord. Wow! When I think about that it just gives me goose bumps; you know the bumps that run down your arms and legs and make your hair stand on end!

Yes, your marriage can glorify God; your relationships can bring Glory to our Saviour!! If we really allow ourselves to think about this and apply it to our relationships we will revolutionize this world we live in. I recently reread the book by Charles Sheldon called, "In His Steps", a timeless classic. The question this humble pastor asked himself, "What would Jesus do?" resounded in his heart and became a part of him. He extended the invitation to his congregation and others made the pledge. This step resulted in extraordinary changes in the way businesses were run and how outreach efforts were conducted. These changes did not come easily and often were the result of personal sacrifices. Money was lost as businesses lost customers who were not in agreement with their new Christian standards. Those in high positions in society had to experience ridicule and sometimes loss of these positions. But the new approach touched and changed lives across the board. Personal sacrifice on the part of these church members helped to obtain Glory for their heavenly Father. Amazing!!!!!

Now picture if we asked this question of ourselves daily, every morning before we start our day. "Is my marriage or relationship glorifying God"? Would that make a difference in our relationships? Most definitely!! Many decisions we make regarding our relationships are self-serving and we set ourselves up for disappointment and failure. If we seek to honour God in our relationships we will make decisions that may require us to deny self and seek the good of the other person.

The greatest example of self-sacrifice is our saviour Jesus Christ who gave up Himself for us all, in spite of all that we have done. He bore all our sins and infirmities upon Himself so we can have forgiveness, the benefit of a personal relationship with Him, and an eternal home. He brought Glory unto His Father. Personal sacrifice may not be easy but it reaps great rewards. *"For when we were still without strength, in due time Christ died for the ungodly. For scarcely for a righteous man will one die; yet perhaps for a good man someone would even dare to die. But God demonstrates His own love towards us, in that while we were still sinners, Christ died for us."* Romans 5:6-8

Let's go back to our illustration of the young couple. The young woman had different ideas of how she wanted to set up their home. A woman is a nurturer and a peacemaker; she loves to create a home as a place of peace and security. She saw the deck in the back as a place to unwind, to re-evaluate and relax. She saw a place where the family could congregate and fellowship together. The big bay windows would draw all the natural light into the home and establish a home filled with warmth and serenity.

It is a part of who she is to think this way and her outlook is not meant to bring conflict. This is a simple illustration of the differences in a male and female relationship. Can such wonderful ideas, each well meaning in their intent work together? Of course they can!

As this young couple heard each other out and each opinion was respected they began to work toward a resolution. The young man saw how important it was for the woman to create a warm and comfortable home for their family. He suggested that they could build two decks, a small one for the front and a larger one for the back. The young woman was warmed by his suggestion and made a suggestion of her own. She suggested that they take time in the morning to have coffee on the front deck together and have a large window facing the front so they can see who is coming onto their property. They were both happy with their decision. When they finally finished building their home and were settled in they woke up the next morning and decided to try out their front deck and have coffee together. They came outside and to their delight they realized that the sun rose in the front of the house in the morning so they could watch the sunrise together. As they praised God together for His amazing love for them and the beauty of the sunset, they began to understand His goodness. They were not only going to enjoy the sun in the morning together but as their work day came to an end and dinner was finished they could see the sunset on their back porch together. That peace the young woman desired was obtained through their mutual agreement and decision. God honoured them and gave them a beautiful sunrise and a beautiful sunset.

There are many important issues to discuss and evaluate before you begin a marriage. Approach your pastor regarding pre-marital counselling and ask for suggestions on good reading material or seminars to attend. Some of the bigger issues that need to be addressed are:

1. Children

How many children are you planning on having? Have you even asked each other that question? What if you discover you are unable to have children then what are your options? Would you both agree on adoption?

Many people feel that they would be "jumping the gun" or acting in a presumptuous manner if they discuss family planning before marriage. The woman may assume that, since she loves her husband, he certainly would want to have four children just like she does. The man may assume that she'll be happy with the one child that he feels will be enough for a family and marriage. What a dilemma! This example could be reversed, or the numbers for the amount of children might be altered, but the general idea would be the same. There is a definite lack of communication and this lack often causes friction in the beginning of a marriage.

Some couples fail to discuss their vision or their family planning desires before entering into the commitment of marriage.

What if the woman doesn't want to have any children and the husband wants a large family? What could happen is that pregnancy prevention methods could be used in secret by the one desiring to not have children and deceit/lies and trickery becomes a foundation early on in the marriage. These are some of the real issues in marriage, and they should be discussed and worked through prior to committing to each other.

It could happen that after one or two children the pressures of child rearing and finances may put you in a different mind set. The former decision to have four children might now seem to be an impossibility or the desire to have a large family might no longer be there. Don't feel guilty or feel like a failure, as long as it is a mutual decision between both husband and wife.

Family planning decisions are not set in stone, but give you a foundation or a place to begin in formulating the vision for your marriage and family.

I have heard of situations where family planning was not discussed before marriage. In one particular instance there was a young woman who married an older man who already had children from a previous marriage that were grown up and not living at home. This young woman loved children and was excited for this next step she had waited so long for. After they were married, she discovered that he could not father children as he had surgery done after his last marriage. Lack of communication before marriage did not prepare this young woman for this disappointment in her life. I am happy to say though that they worked through this issue and have a successful marriage and are working together in ministry. This is just an example of how two people can enter into a lifelong commitment and have to face obstacles that could have been discussed and resolved from the start.

My husband and I were fortunate to have premarital counselling and did discuss this important issue. We both wanted five or six children but ended up having seven. We both wanted a large family and we are blessed by our children. It brings to mind one of my favourite scriptures. *"Behold children are a heritage from the Lord, the fruit of the womb is a reward. Like arrows in the hand of a warrior, so are the children of ones' youth. Happy is the man who has his quiver full of them; they shall not be ashamed, but speak with their enemies in the gate."* Psalm 127:3-5

When God made a covenant with Adam and Eve it contained two different provisions. One provision was to have **dominion**. *"Let Us make man in Our Image, according to Our likeness; let them have dominion over the fish of the sea, over the birds of the air, and over every creeping thing that creeps on the earth."* Genesis 1:26

This meant they were to be God's kingdom agent, to rule and subdue the earth. Man's ability to sustain his role as ruler of this earth will depend on his obedience and faithfulness to his maker.

The second provision was to have **descendants**. *"Then God blessed them, and God said to them, be fruitful and multiply; fill the earth and subdue it; have dominion over the fish of the sea, over the birds of the air and over every living thing that moves on the earth."* Genesis 1:28. They were to be fruitful and multiply!

These two provisions though very different in nature, must work together to fulfill this covenant. Adam and Eve alone could not take dominion of the earth. It would require their descendants – yes, their children.

To love and care for children is one of the most important ways for us to honour God.

Therefore we honour God when we make wise decisions concerning planning for a family as part of our preparation for marriage.

2. DISCIPLINE

When you have your children how are you going to discipline them? Do you believe in discipline and what methods would you use? Do you both agree to support each other in disciplinary actions?

This is a big one! Society today tells us to be a friend to our children. Let them make their own decisions; give them freedom and space to grow and learn. I hope you realize that our children do not need another friend. They need a mother or father, someone who cares enough about them to give them rules to abide by and boundaries to protect them. They need to know that there is someone at home who cares enough to be concerned where they are at 10 o'clock at night. They need to know there is someone who will make the decisions for them concerning their welfare because they really don't want that responsibility. They don't have to make the choice of whether they should go to a party or not because they already have a rule in place at home that says they are not allowed.

Some parents allow their children to make decisions that they are too young and immature to make and they will pay for their poor choices. Is that taking responsibility away from them? No! It is teaching them by our rules how to make responsible decisions at an early age and then formatting a pattern for them to make the right choices when they are old enough to do so.

Our first child was born into this world screaming. She let the whole world know that she arrived and was now a vital part of society. Her voice must be heard. The next couple months we walked, jiggled, threw her over our lap, patted her back, and fed her hourly to try to stop the constant crying. She was labelled a colicky baby and I was told this would last at least the first five months of her new life. She was passed from hand to willing hand; all tried bravely to ease her discomfort and tears. I saw the brightly covered walls of our church nursery as a second home as her loud cry interrupted many church services. As soon as she turned 5 months old, I kid you not, the crying stopped. I enjoyed the next few precious months as our daughter transformed before our eyes with her quick quirky smiles and deep throated laughter. As she began to discover the wonderful world of taking her first steps and venturing into the unknown we began to notice a stubborn streak appearing now and again. Thus began our journey of shaping and formatting principles and disciplinary measures that would anchor our family unit and carry through to all the children.

The first important step in administering discipline is allowing God to be your starting point. When you build a foundation of discipline in your home you need somewhere to begin and God needs to be first and foremost in that process. The next step is then to examine your character. We learn a lot about others around us by observing their characteristics. Children are constantly mimicking those closest to them and those they spend the most time with. Their minds are developing at a rapid pace in the first five years of their lives. We can see how they learn by our examples and our attitudes. Are we exhibiting godly attitudes in our home? It is easy to exhibit godly attitudes in our churches but what about in our community or our own home? Our life in Christ needs to flow out of the four church walls and into the community. I try to check my spiritual life regularly in terms of the effect I am having in the community. Are people noticing that our family is different or are we blending into the crowd doing what every other parents are doing or saying?

We live in a close knit community where there are a lot of young families and the community is small enough where people know your name or at least recognize you and greet you. I have noticed that people are observing our large family and generally have many questions to ask of me. They will make favourable comments about our children and their attitudes and nature. These are all opportunities to give credit to God and His standard for raising children. We really don't realize how much people are watching and observing us.

One woman in our church once approached my oldest daughter at choir practice. She proceeded to share with her that when she first came to the church she was blessed observing our family of nine sitting together and worshipping the Lord. She said this was one of the reasons she decided to attend this church. We would have never known this if she had not told us. It makes you think about others that are watching and observing as well and we may never know the impact we have made on their lives. Only God will know but He receives the glory for this and that is our reward!

What about in our homes? What attitudes and behaviours are we exhibiting? How can we expect our children to respect others if respect is not shown to each other in the home? I have noticed that at times when I have let disappointment and frustration get the best of me and have allowed myself to voice these opinions that my children at times have picked up on these views. I hear my own frustration become a part of their speech and actions. I am horrified at what I have done and try my best to correct my mistake and apologize to them for my words, sharing the appropriate ways I should have dealt with the situation. No, we are not perfect and we will make mistakes along the way but it's what we do with those mistakes that make the difference. Children need to see their parents modelling forgiveness. Our children can respect us for being honest with them and in turn respect God because He is always honest with them. The Bible tells us, *"The righteous man walks in his integrity; His children are blessed after him."* Proverbs 20:7 NKJV

When we are consistent in our discipline we will reap success. The moment you give in to their complaints and veer away from your original plan of discipline you are opening yourself to disaster. I know that when I am tired and have had a busy day I often would rather avoid a problem than have to deal with it. But I have learned by experience and painful lessons that avoidance will only allow the problem to grow bigger and lack of discipline will unravel the very cord you have secured them with in the first place. A good example would be our

TV rule. We have made a rule in our home that TV is only allowed on the weekend. The week days and evenings should be focused on schoolwork but the weekend is family time and TV would be allowed. Before I knew it, a show was being watched here and there while I was away. "But I was finished my homework Mom!" was the common reply. I let it go a few times but then discovered that they were taking more liberties concerning the TV. It didn't bother them anymore because I never directly addressed the issue. My failure in addressing this gave them the liberty to continue to watch more shows while I was away. It went even as far as me coming home and finding them watching a show with no indication of guilt or shame. I had to pull up my own socks and be more consistent in the rules we made together as a family and be an example to my own children.

Did you hear that? I said the rules we made together as a family. I have learned from many failed attempts of trying to institute rules that I felt were vital to the family that if the children are a part of formulating the rules they will more likely stick to them. It is also a part of creating respect amongst each other and caring enough to allow them to have their say and part in structuring the home. Healthy respect of each member in the household no matter their age is necessary. Each member plays an important role in the home.

3. FINANCES

Besides infidelity, money problem is one of the leading causes of divorce today. The stress it can put on a marriage is tremendous.

Who is going to be the main provider for the family? Are you both in agreement concerning work whether one parent should stay home to be the caregiver for the children? Who will be the one taking care of the bills? What about savings, do you both think it's important?

These are important questions that you need to ask each other before the wedding day, while you are planning your future together. Otherwise you may receive a big shock after the honeymoon. Concerning finances, my husband and I were not too prepared as we should have been. My husband had come to Canada on his own when he was just seventeen years old and independently worked on getting his work permit and citizenship. He shared with me once how he remembers getting a roll of quarters, going to a phone booth and calling all the lawyers he could find in the telephone book. He worked hard as a young man and with God's help and his hard work he established himself in Canada.

Now saying all that, this determined young man was very careful with his money. He started a saving account with the little he could accumulate. Then he met the woman he had prayed for (that's me!) and started to prepare for marriage. He intentionally did not share the fact that he had a savings account. He allowed his future wife to assume that he had just a small amount of money in the bank. One of his main reasons for doing so was that he observed that his bride-to-be liked to shop. He was worried that I might spend all his hard earned money so he intentionally hid that account from me. As we established our relationship after the wedding he realized that he should not keep this from me anymore and that it was wrong to keep this a secret. I was pretty surprised when he told me but was too happy to know that we had some savings put aside to get angry with him. It helped me to look at my spending and shopping habits and learn to be more economical.

Some couples enter into marriage with preconceived ideas concerning the woman's role and the man's role in providing for the family. A woman who has worked in a satisfying career for many years before meeting the man of her dreams might be surprised to find out that after marriage her husband expects her to stay home and is adamant about it. Or a woman who expects to stay at home and raise children might be shocked to find out she is expected to work full time and the tables turn. I am not saying that these roles cannot be worked out but they should not be assumed. All this needs to be discussed before marriage so a compromise can be reached between the two individuals.

I love being a homemaker but there were times where financially I needed to contribute and work outside of the home. This is all part of raising a family and addressing the different needs a family has. But assuming and expecting roles to be played according to your desires will only cause havoc and confusion. Discussing these important issues before marriage will help you to work out your differences and come to a conclusion about how you will manage your home.

I dislike handling finances and have reluctantly been the main person in our relationship to do so. But I see the responsibility my husband has in the many jobs and ministries he has to manage. To be able to ease some of that pressure off his shoulders has become a blessing to me. If I were to add this extra responsibility on his busy plate I will definitely not reap the blessings of appreciation and love he shows towards me. It will also take away his valuable free time and instead it can be directed to me and the children.

The expectations we place on each other as individuals can cause tremendous pressure. If we take time to talk about these issues before marriage we avoid a lot of road blocks in our relationships.

I love this quote from a very well known woman of God, Ruth Bell Graham.

"It is a foolish woman who expects her husband to be to her that which only Jesus Christ Himself can be: always ready to forgive, totally understanding, unendingly patient, invariably tender and loving, unfailing in every area, anticipating every need, and making more than adequate provision. Such expectations put a man under impossible strain… The same goes for the man who expects too much from his wife." [1]

Points to Ponder:

- *What are some things you can do to prepare yourself for beginning a relationship or preparing for marriage?*

- *How can discussing future plans concerning children prepare you for your relationship or marriage?*

- *Who administers discipline in your marriage? What or who should be the foundation for your plan of discipline?*

- *Who is your ultimate source for finance?*

- *What expectations do you place on each other that could ultimately destroy your relationship?*

4 HELLO WORLD

One of our bible school students came up to me one day and shared that he felt his particular culture needed teaching on living a real and practical life. He realized that many of his fellow Christians were strong in prayer and the spiritual side of life but did not know how to translate it into living an effective and practical life here on earth. It kind of confirmed my feelings regarding our marriages today. We have many preconceived ideas about how marriage should be and think that the "feeling of love" will bring us through any and every situation we face.

Our marriage should be lived with the same practicality as our Christian walk. Christ has called us to walk this Christian life as He did while on this earth. He experienced hunger, loss of friends and loved ones, betrayal, and much more. But He did not beam Himself up to heaven to escape the tribulations He had to face. He lived a humble but effective life while here on earth. Yes, Jesus did great miracles as well and we saw the supernatural pulled down into the natural, but it was balanced with living a basic human life. Many storms and adversities will try to pull down our marriages but it is all part and package of living a practical life today.

I wish I could tell you that marriage is a bed of roses and weeds will never arise amidst its lush beauty. Marriage is more than the feeling of love. My husband told me shortly after we were married that he chose to love me. At first I was a little miffed at him, thinking well, that's not very romantic. He chose to love me? What does that mean? Does he not feel anything for me? What about all the butterflies in the stomach and the secret smiles and the tingles up and down the spine? Does his choice do away with all that? Well the more I thought about it the deeper it sank in. This man loves me even when the anger is there or the butterflies are not fluttering. He loves me when the walls seem like they are closing in and the problems of this life try to extinguish the flame of desire. He does not base his love on the feelings or circumstances; he chooses to love me through it all. Now doesn't that sound romantic? This is a love that will stand the test of time.

The bed of roses takes some pruning and planting. It takes some rooting out and pulling down to produce a healthy bush. In order to see the beauty of the roses we have to get past the thorns and cut away the unhealthy branches. The rose then unfurls its petals and all can admire the beauty and fragrance of that rose bush. That bed of roses produces something wonderful but it takes work to bring it to that point. We need to ask ourselves what our marriage is portraying to the world around us. Do people notice the beauty of our relationships or has the rose lost its fragrance?

I had a rose bush that was left unattended for a whole summer because our front walkway was being paved that summer. The contractor was putting our job on the back burner because of previous commitments so we were stuck the entire summer with a very unattractive front yard. That rose bush we had left unattended grew very long scraggly branches that would at times reach out and grab you as you walked by. The roses themselves were nothing to look at and often were ignored by passersby. It actually was very annoying and the rosebush itself was look upon as a nuisance.

Today we see many marriages that are falling apart because they have not been attended to. The world is looking at us to show a true example of a godly marriage. Are they looking at us in disgust and saying, "That is not attractive, why would I want to get married and look that way!" Or are they saying, "Wow, look at the strength and beauty of that marriage; I pray I can have that for myself; I wonder how they achieved that?"

Marriage has been getting a bad rap for way too long. The next generation of marriage potentials are backing away from marriage and commitment. Our young people are looking at us and shaking their heads. Statistics tell us that "30 years ago men and women were eloping at a median of 23.2 and 20.8 years of age, according to the U.S. census Bureau. In 2006, those numbers have increased to 27.5 and 25.5 respectively." [2]

What has distracted our youth from entering into the covenant of marriage? Some say women's movements have devalued the traditional views of marriage. Others say that the media has a great influence as it tends to portray family relationships as a battle ground full of negative and harmful situations. On the other hand, the media portrays the single life as a glamorous free life. The emphasis is on personal fulfillment and personal gain.

If one was raised amidst divorce and had to endure some form of separation from a parent one may have reservations toward marriage. One thing I have learned is that we need to decide for ourselves what a godly marriage and a godly family entail. We do not have to allow our past and our parents' past mistakes haunt us and allow our view of marriage to be below standard. We do not need to be the statistical norm; instead, we should fight to raise the standard and purity of marriage.

Besides being blessed by God for honouring our marriage vows there are definite physical benefits of a healthy marriage.

Benefits for Women

There are many physical benefits for women who are in a healthy marriage relationship. Women are generally physically and emotionally healthier. They are less at risk of attempting or committing suicide. If feelings of depression or stress try to hinder a woman she has her spouse to help encourage her and bring her through it.

They are less at risk of contracting sexual diseases or struggling with drug and alcohol abuse. When you are committed in a relationship you are committed to one partner so therefore the risk of contracting sexual diseases is not a factor. A spouse will encourage correct behaviour and avoidance of consumption of things that would not benefit their relationship or foster good health.

Women have more stability concerning finances and have better relationships with their children. In fact, they have more satisfying relationships all around. When you know that you are supported and loved by another it extends to your children and those around you. It will have a domino effect where it touches all those in your circle, even your community.

I feel the need to also tell you that all the health benefits of marriage are consistent across age, race and education groups. As we begin to discuss the benefits for men and children we need to know that these benefits cover all these groups. You cannot say that your culture or age diminishes these benefits. It crosses all barriers and touches all ages. Going through different surveys, whether Christian or not, they all give the same facts.

BENEFITS FOR MEN

Men share many of the same benefits that women have concerning a healthy marriage. They are physically and emotionally healthier. They have less risk of drug and alcohol abuse or attempts of suicide. When men live alone they take more risks because they do not have anyone relying on them or partnering with them to see to their health.

Men who are married have less risk of contracting sexual diseases. They also have stronger sexual satisfaction. Married men actually have more sex than single men. Since sexual satisfaction is one of men's top needs, a married man is more fulfilled and satisfied in this area.

Married men also have employment stability and with that come higher wages. Why is that? Employers see stability and responsibility when it comes to hiring a family man. Tax breaks and government assistance is also greater when considering a married man.

Relationships concerning children are stronger and vibrant in a marriage setting. There is peace and security on the child's side so it will extend to their relationship with their father. Married men also excel in their relationships with others as trust and commitment are seen by their friends and community.

Men are statistically proven to live longer when married. The rate of mortality is more than double among single men. When men struggle with health issues like cancer for example, their recovery rate is much higher if they are married. Twice as much time is spent in the hospital by unmarried people than their married peers.

Married people are generally happier than unmarried people of the same age. Research indicates that married people are healthier as well which would account for their happiness.

Marriage offers a man the kind of stability and support that allows him to succeed in all the different areas of life. If you really take time to think about it, how much more could you accomplish with the presence of a loving and caring spouse?

BENEFITS FOR CHILDREN

A healthy marriage holds many benefits for children as well. In a strong family unit a child is less likely to engage in delinquent behaviours or develop an addiction to drugs and alcohol. There is less risk of becoming pregnant as a teen or becoming sexually active. When the child is not engaging in sexual activity he/she will also avoid contracting sexual diseases.

Children from a healthy marriage are more likely to attend college and succeed academically. Having the support of both a mother and a father in the home creates an atmosphere for children to be emotionally and physically healthier. Family dynamics between child and father or child and mother are less likely to be stressful and more likely to be stronger in a healthy marriage setting. Seeing their parents working together in their marriage and succeeding will also decrease children's chances of divorcing when they are in a marriage relationship themselves.

Not only does a healthy marriage affect the individual families members involved but it also provides benefits for communities. God's plan for marriages is to affect society on the whole and bring blessing to the whole community.

BENEFITS FOR COMMUNITIES

If we take into consideration all the benefits a healthy marriage has for men, women and children we will understand that this will affect the community in a very positive way. Healthy families will create more physically and emotionally healthy citizens. There will also be a higher rate of educated citizens.

We will see the rate of domestic violence drop drastically and crime rate will be reduced as well. The need for social services will decrease as families work together in their family unit and then help those around them to do the same.

Marriage helps create better and more reliable employees, increase earnings, and increase property values. If only our communities could take a deeper look into the great benefits they reap from healthier marriages I think they would invest more into this diamond mine. [3]

We need a wake up call today in our marriages and in our relationships. We need to say "HELLO WORLD, THIS IS ME AND THIS IS WHAT A MARRIAGE IS SUPPOSED TO LOOK LIKE". Are you ready for that challenge? Challenges will come from every side but it's what you do with them that will make the real difference. We need to wake up and see each new day as a valuable gift from God.

Points to Ponder

- *A healthy marriage takes work. Have you come from a background of broken relationships? Is it possible to break this pattern? What have you done recently to break the cycle?*

- *Think of a few ways that your marriage has brought benefits to you as a man or woman. Does doing this help you appreciate your spouse and all the benefits your relationship brings to you?*

- *Focus on the positive aspects of your relationship today. Encourage your spouse by expressing how much you appreciate him or her.*

- *Know that challenges will come but with God's help and your determination to work through them the challenges will build character in you, empowering you for the next step in your relationship.*

5 MOTHERHOOD OR WOMANHOOD

MOTHERHOOD

The biggest challenge I had to face in my personal life as a woman was the balance between motherhood and womanhood. I struggled with and still struggle finding my place as a woman in my home. The demands of a busy home often infringe on your personal development. As a mother I am usually busy managing the family and the individual needs of each child. Being a mother of seven has left little room for anything else.

There is much joy in sowing into these little ones' lives and seeing the rewards of your labour. When they are small you are wiping noses, rocking cradles, pacing floors, doing endless laundry and dishes. Your world grows smaller as the demands on your time are limited to these delightful gifts from God. Their tiny fingers wrap around yours and they simply trust and love you unconditionally. As they giggle and marvel at the world around them, your heart fills up to overflowing with the blessing of it all. It is a wonderful gift from God to experience motherhood and all the benefits attached to it.

Paul tell us when describing his ministry to the Thessalonians, "… *but we were gentle among you, just as a nursing mother cherishes her own children. So affectionately longing for you, we were well pleased to impart to you not only the gospel of God, but also our own lives, because you had become so dear to us.*" I Thess. 2:7-8 "Cherish" literally means "to hold and treat as dear." It involved nurturing and tender care. A mother instinctively longs to press her child to herself, protecting him or her from

danger, soothing their hurts and easing their pain.

It is second nature to us and as we draw our children near to us we fulfill our mandate as a mother. "*Behold, children are a heritage from the Lord; the fruit of the womb is a reward*". Psalm 127:3

Everything which we value, or which we desire, is a gift from God, and is to be received as from Him, and to be acknowledged as His gift. Children are one of the divine favours bestowed on us by God. This includes their lives, their health, their virtues, and the happiness we receive from them. Not only is it a joy to be a mother but it is a reward from our heavenly Father. We should feel privileged to have this honour of raising these precious gifts of God.

At times we forget that our children are a heritage from the Lord. When I was looking up the word "heritage" in the dictionary it told me that one of meanings of this word is "something reserved for one". God has reserved this inheritance for you and me. It is exclusively yours; no one has the right to this child but you. It is our "portion" from the Lord. I don't know about you but if God has given me my children as a "portion" an exclusive gift from God's throne room, I would honour and treasure this heavenly treasure.

I have always had a hard time hearing people complain about their children. It's like saying, "God, you didn't know what you were doing the day you gave me this child! What were you thinking?" We moan and complain about all the duties we have to fulfill as a parent and those around us get the idea that being a mother is one big and horrible chore. We often make it seem as if children are nothing more than a burden to an already busy life.

It is easy to get caught up in this cycle and that is why it is important to surround ourselves with positive role models and strong family units. I know that when I have had a very busy day I sometimes feel like unloading my worst moments on to the next person I talk to, especially if they are bemoaning their busy day and they haven't experienced half of what I had to deal with that day. I feel like screaming, "That's all you have to deal with, one child? Try seven of them." I try to avoid such conversations but if they do come up I work on changing the negative words into words of encouragement and positive thoughts. I have learned to take my frustrations out on my husband instead. Just kidding!!! I take my frustrations to the Lord and have a heart to heart talk with Him. He alone can understand the difficulties we face and He can give us encouragement and strength.

The Bible tells us, "Now that we have received, not the spirit of the world, but the Spirit which is of God; that we might know the things that are freely given to us of God." I Corinthians 2:12 His Spirit makes known to us His will and the things that are freely given to us of God. Through His Spirit I can be led to understanding and strength for another day. Not only that but He fills me with His joy and I can again rejoice in my role as a mother.

As an adjective, "motherhood" means "having or relating to an inherent worthiness, justness or goodness this is obvious or unarguable." [4]

Motherhood is nothing to be ashamed of or to be degraded. We have inherent worthiness and it is obvious to those around us. No one can argue that it is any different! We have been called to a higher calling, and it's found in motherhood!

Enjoy some quotes on motherhood.

"Only God Himself fully appreciates the influence
of a Christian mother in the moulding of character in her children."
— **Billy Graham**

"A mother's love's a blessing, no matter where you roam
Keep her while she's living, you'll miss her when she's gone
Love her as in childhood, though feeble, old and grey
For you'll never miss a mother's love, till she's buried beneath the clay."
— **Thomas P. Keen**

WOMANHOOD

When I was sharing with my husband my different ideas regarding chapters for this book I mentioned the motherhood or womanhood chapter. He asked a very common question. What's the difference?

Well there is a big difference and I feel it is a very important topic to discuss. Womanhood is different in its function and definition. The definition of womanhood is "the state of being a woman; the distinguishing character or qualities of a woman, or of womankind". [4] Womanhood therefore describes the characteristics of an individual woman and her unique God-given qualities. Each of us was created with gifting and characteristics that form who we are as a person. Being a woman is more than just motherhood; it is all the personality and qualities we bring to this world. As an individual person we need to allow God to work through us with the gifting He has placed in us. We are responsible to fulfill the call He places upon our life.

I mentioned earlier that I personally struggle in the area of developing my womanhood without getting lost in the role of motherhood. I feel that in today's society many women are feeling the same way. We have become so busy trying to be the perfect mother and meeting all the expectations of a mother today that are pretty impossible to meet, that we can lose ourselves in the role. We sacrifice time and time again on behalf of the family but at the cost of our own personal growth. Then we wonder why we are feeling depressed, tired and a little lost. It's a little like being under water, fighting for your last breath, then you surface again for a short time but before you know it you are under water again.

I struggle with this as I try to balance a large family, each with their own needs and challenges. Their needs often fill each day from morning to night and I'm sometimes unable to accomplish every task so things get be carried over to the next day. Most days you will find me waking up running and falling in bed exhausted. This has led in the past, to my personal time with the Lord being sporadic - a hit and miss according to how busy the day would be. I started to live my life around the children and my husband and my life became robotic; my passion began to dwindle and my joy faded into a pale reflection of my former self.

God began to speak to me concerning my role as a woman. It incorporated not only motherhood but many more exciting aspects. In fact if I did not embrace or challenge myself in other areas I would surely burn out in my role as a mother. I would like to share some of these areas with you as we learn together how to develop our womanhood.

1. Personal Relationship with Jesus

One of the first things I was challenged on was my personal relationship with Jesus.

I remember when my husband and I were in the early years of our marriage. He went to bible school and both of us worked, struggling to raise a young family. Wonderful years really! We saw God's hand of provision time and time again as He met all our needs. But one thing that really stood out to me those years was my dependence on my husband to grow in my walk with the Lord. I pushed him ahead towards ministry but yet I hid behind him when he ministered. He was growing in leaps and bounds and I was happily supporting him as a wife but never allowing God to use me for Himself. I was blinded to this fact and it never bothered me that I was known as "Harrison's wife" because people would forget my name but they all knew Him. He started early morning prayer in our home and in school during his bible school years and ended up being the school valedictorian on graduation day. I was and still am very proud of him.

We began to tour after school and I was happily tagging along with the kids, visiting all the nurseries and washrooms across Canada trying to keep them happy and quiet during ministry time. I remember one time when the Holy Spirit was moved so strongly in a wonderful church in Swift Current, Saskatchewan. It was very quiet as the Spirit moved and the children were fussing. The church did not have a nursery or class room, only a one person bathroom. I went in there with the children and spent hours keeping them quiet until the service was finished. The memories of beginning in ministry are wonderful really, a time of growth and yet so much expectation.

Then we moved to Split, Croatia, a beautiful country with the Adriatic Sea on one side and snow covered mountains on the other. Although the country was beautiful it was being torn apart by war on either side. We arrived with three small children and were introduced to the church that same night; the next morning we were left on our own in a small apartment in the city. We did not know the language and there were only a few young people in the church who could speak a bit of English. It was definitely a challenge for us, especially my husband as he went out every day, evangelizing, making connections and getting to know the people and culture there. I was home with our three children, all under the age of three, every day from early morning till evening when my husband would stumble through the door exhausted and practically fall into bed. I did not know anyone and my world was those small mouldy walls of the apartment. We would often wake up during the night to gunfire outside. When we asked one of our young church members about it they would causally reply, "Oh, it's probably just a drunk soldier."

During this time period I would often feel lonely and had time to fill besides coloring pages and pages of colouring books with the girls. I began to read my Bible more and just out of boredom I hate to say. But I began to grow and mature as a Christian and as a woman of God. I began to receive comfort and strength from the Word of God and as I continued to read, it began to prepare me for the things He would ask me to do for His name. I will never forget our sweet communion together in those earlier days as God began to show Himself to me and I found my personal worth through fellowship with Him. God showed me that I had gifting I could impart to those hurting around me and I could support my husband and ministry in many more ways than I had before.

2. PERSONAL MINISTRY

As I was absorbing the Word, God began to move in other ways than just through His Word. He started to give me opportunities to step out and use His Word. I remember clearly one evening when my husband came home from a very trying day. We finally settled ourselves in bed and as I started to drift off into dream land I received a small nudge at my side. My husband was trying to get my attention. He could not move and felt as if there was a heavy weight upon him so that even his words were being forced out as his lips felt the same weight. Without thinking I began to pray loudly with great confidence coming against the spirit that was binding him. Gradually the weight lifted off of him and he could move again.

My husband was very shocked by my prayers; I believe he thought he was dreaming. I had never done that before, but it came without thinking because I had been pouring the Word inside of me. God was moving so that even I was not aware of what had happened until it was finished. Wow! My husband still talks about this experience and it really was a starting point for our ministry together.

My husband began to slowly push me out of my comfort zone and started to create opportunities for me to minister. Suddenly he was too tired to go to prayer meeting, how about I go in his place and let him rest. After a few times of doing this I suddenly discovered I was going to be teaching some bible school classes to fill a great need for training of these wonderful young people. Then at one point my husband was so exhausted one Sunday morning, he just said, "You can preach for me. I just can't go today." Well this was a little bit much for me. But I couldn't refuse; he went out all day and every evening doing meetings and evangelism. It really caught up with him that morning. Very reluctantly I took the bus to our church which was meeting at that time in a very small space close to a small shopping area. I don't remember what I preached on and all the details of that Sunday but I know I experienced an amazing release of self dependence and I was finally able to allow God to lead me.

I discovered that God had equipped me as a woman of God with many important qualities that needed to be developed. It was a process for me and as I strengthened my personal relationship with God and expanded my personal ministry I became a much more effective mother. My life was not my own anymore, where I could just choose to remain in one area and never step beyond the boundaries I had made for myself. If I wanted to excel in motherhood I needed to excel in my womanhood. What example would I be for my children if my own expectations for myself were limited? They needed to see me progress and challenge myself, trying something new, developing the gifts that

God had given me. If my children need a hero, a role model to follow, they need to find it in my husband and me, aside from their ultimate hero of course, Jesus Christ.

3. PERSONAL LIFE

We all need some form of tension releasing activity. There must be a balance between your spiritual walk and taking care of yourself physically. As a mother the physical stressors can be overwhelming and if you don't make room for some down time on your own or with your husband you could crash. God has created us with physical needs and desires. If we continue to ignore our own needs we will come to the point where we will wear out and become no use at all to anyone, especially our children.

I can always tell when I am reaching that point of stress, where the children's voices become shriller and louder and all reasoning seems to fly out the window. Everyone's demands seem to be brought to me at the same time and nothing I say seems to be effective; its time to stop, re-evaluate and cool-down. Each person is different in the way they effectively refuel and recharge. I love to take a long bath and read a good book, or go for a walk if the weather is nice.

What is your outlet for relaxation and stimulation? You need to fit it into your schedule no matter how busy you are. Often through these activities we form new relationships and can open new doors of opportunity for ministry.

Don't lose yourself in the roles that others expect of you. People around you can be your own worst enemy even though they may mean well. I have had friends tell me that I take on too much, and that I need to spend more time at home. Some even ask how is it possible to raise a family and do what I do. Well, we do have to be careful to balance our lives but we cannot settle ourselves in one role and let the seed that was planted in our heart lie dormant. Eventually our own branch grafted into the true vine will become bare and withered.

God has so much in store for each and every woman who desires to bear much fruit. I love being a mother and never regret one moment of the time and energy I have sown into my family. God has unique callings and giftings for each of us and we are allowed to lengthen our perimeters and step out of the boundaries we may have put up for ourselves concerning our role as a mother and as a woman.

Queen Esther could have nicely settled in her role of a queen, quietly raise her family in the palace and continue to have great success in doing that but she had a calling, a purpose to fulfill as a woman of God. She was called to take a stand for her people, to save a nation, and to deliver them from sure death.

We may have a calling outside our home's four walls, something bigger than ourselves, something only God can do through a willing and yielded vessel. The devil would love for us to stay settled in one place, living our own happy lives and allowing our branches to be barren. When you crack a branch that has lain dormant for a season you will notice the inside has become dry and brittle and the strength of that branch has diminished. It may even have become rotten inside if it has been away from the strength of the vine for too long. We all need to be refilled and then produce again to be a fruitful branch of our wonderful Saviour, Jesus, the true vine.

Points to Ponder:

- *Do you struggle in balancing who you are as a mother and as a woman? How can you be both successfully?*

- *Why do we bury ourselves in only one role and then are afraid to step out in the other? Do we limit ourselves to only what we know we can do?*

- *Have you allowed others to discourage you or diminish your role as a woman or as a mother? Remember that you are tapped into the vine of our Saviour Jesus Christ who supplies our branches with life giving strength so that we will be able to bear our fruit in its season.*

6 100 Reasons to Love, Respect and Admire Your Spouse

"Live joyfully with the wife whom you love all the days of your vain life which He has given you under the sun, all the days of vanity, for that is your portion in life, and in the labor which you perform under the sun." Ecclesiastes 9:9

This year something happened in my relationship with my husband that caused me to re-evaluate myself and the different ways I interact with him on a personal level. It shook me up and brought me to a breaking point in my life as a woman and wife. I realized that I have failed in many areas of support concerning him personally, not relating to the children or work or home but him alone. I had thought I was supporting him in all the ways possible but unintentionally I was doing the opposite.

Men have a very strong need to be respected and admired. This does not just come by doing all the right things like cooking and cleaning; it takes your total attention to be focused on him as a person. He needs to be seen as more than just a provider, a father, a husband. He needs to be seen as an individual separate from all the responsibilities he has.

As I began to think about my husband in this different light, I decided to write down 100 reasons why I love, respect and admire him. I left the house one morning after all the children went to school and bought a coffee at the local McDonald's. I brought my computer with me and sat down to begin my list. This was my way of accomplishing what I set out to do, for remaining at home holds too many distractions for me. I think about putting in a load of wash, or cleaning that front hallway. Or, what about those dishes in the sink and let's not forget getting some baking done. So I found a place away from those distractions.

At first I thought I would have a difficult time writing 100 reasons. I took a few sips of my coffee, stared at the computer screen for a few minutes then began to type.

2. You taught me how to loosen up and laugh more.

I can take myself way too seriously and my husband has helped me to laugh more, at myself and at the situations that seem to be bigger than they are. I wrote nine more, and then decided to group them in ten. I breezed through the next ten, and the more I wrote, the more things I remembered and realized I admired and respected my husband for. I thought about who he is to me as a husband, a lover, a friend.

11. You write loving messages on my bathroom mirror

12. You don't complain about my cold feet.

I thought about the tender moments of family time and the impact he has had on our children.

21. Seeing you play with the kids

22. Staying up late, helping them with their essays.

23. Planning girls' or boys' night out

Then I thought about all the accomplishments he has achieved over the years I have known him and the progression he has made from year to year.

29. Earning two masters and a doctorate.

30. Cheating sleep to accomplish these goals

I thought about the sacrifices he has made for me and our children so we can have what we have today. I also thought about the encouragement he has been to our children concerning education and future advancement.

32. Seeing and planning educationally for the kids when I don't see it.

34. Challenging all of us to push harder and reach for the stars

My fingers flew over the keyboard only stopping for another sip or coffee here and there. I added some more.

45. You respect and honour your parents and mine.

48. You respect your body and take care of it, setting a good example.

I thought about all the positive attributes of his character and how that has benefited our family and others who come across his pathway.

65. Never allowed negative words or people to pull you down

81. People's lives are changed and marriages saved because of you.

His fun nature and creativity keeps me guessing and life is never dull or boring, to say the least.

84. Taught me how to dance the salsa.

96. Sets the atmosphere for romance and intrigue.

Before I knew it, I had 100 reasons.

I could have written more. I will write more, but I had accomplished what I had set out to do, and I did it in less than an hour. Writing this list opened my eyes to see what I had been missing all these years. I had missed opportunities to share how I feel about him. I had also lost special moments because I just expected him to function in his role in the home. These expectations had fostered frustration and separated us from relating to each other as unique and vulnerable human beings.

When we just function in the roles we have been assigned, life becomes dull. It becomes a boring routine where we go through the motions of doing what is expected of us, reaping maybe a few back slaps of good work here and there but some achievements generally go unnoticed. The person we want to hear the encouragement, the praise, the tender words, and the tender touch from is our spouse. It doesn't just happen when we share a few happy moments in the bedroom or a few dates here and there. It happens when we acknowledge small feats, when we whisper in their ears something that we love about them this can carry them through their day as they remember your words.

It happens when we steal a kiss, or catch their eye and send a special message through them. It happens when we see that they have had a rough day and ask them what has happened. This can be followed up with patient listening without judgement, and without thought of what you need to do at that moment. Putting your spouse before all your other responsibilities at that time so that they feel special, wanted, needed and heard is important. Too many times we find all the excuses and jobs that need to be accomplished and put them ahead of our spouse. It is not always done intentionally. We feel justified in our role as mother and homemaker that all that we do is more important than that moment of serving or listening to our spouse.

We only fool ourselves and end up losing far more than we can imagine. I have learned that the small sacrifices we make for our relationship are bricks on which we build our marriage. My eyes are opening more to the needs of my spouse as I see the impact it is making on our own relationship. I am not sure if you have heard of the saying, "Rome was not built in one day." Well, it is the same with a marriage. Marriage and our relationships are built brick by brick, experience upon experience, sacrifice upon sacrifice. Too many times we focus on the negative aspects of our relationship and we delay or stop the building process.

My husband and I have talked to and counselled many couples who struggle with the little irritations of their relationship with their spouse. They may seem trivial or silly in some people's eyes but are very real to the couple who is dealing with it. Many people just can't get past the very real and conflicting differences men and women have. I guarantee you 100 % that you will not find a spouse who feels and does things exactly the way you do. It is impossible, for we were created unique and totally different in our characteristics and personalities. Most women when asked to describe their perfect mate or the characteristics they wish to see their mate exhibit, they end up describing another woman. Why is that? Because they have not learned that men are very different in characteristic and nature than women.

God in His wisdom created man and woman and was very strategic in how He did so. God does nothing by chance or whim. He knew exactly what He was doing and we need to understand that. We cannot change our spouse especially when it has to do with their inherent nature that was given to them from the beginning of time. When we begin to understand the dynamics of relationships we will understand God's divine wisdom in creating men and women as He did. Marriage is a beautiful thing to behold when a couple understands and respects each other's differences.

I believe one of the key elements in building a relationship is looking at ourselves first before we point the finger at our spouse. When we point our finger at our spouse accusing them of all the fault in our relationship we need to realize that we have four more fingers and they are pointing intentionally back at us. What are we doing about it? It takes an intentional act of looking at our part in the relationship to see what we are doing to make it better, and what we have done that may have brought about the disagreement. It takes two to tangle, and we are responsible to

God to check our heart and our intentions, that they are from a pure motive or intention.

When God talks about the relationship between a husband and wife He tells the husband to love his wife. Why? This is because a woman is very emotionally driven and when a husband loves his wife, he is touching her emotions and fulfilling her greatest need as a woman. This is her need to feel connected with her husband based on her feelings. I know from experiencing this as a wife and soul mate. When we share our feelings and love for one another we create a soul tie that is not easily broken. If we are aware of the seriousness of this act we will create something so wonderful and so strong that nothing will be able to tear or destroy this relationship.

Trouble comes when we are not meeting each other's needs, or are unaware what each others needs are. The enemy is waiting just outside the circle we have created as a husband and wife and as a family. He is looking for any kinks or broken cords to get through that would give him an opportunity to mess with us.

There is a lady in our church who prays for our family on a regular basis. It touches my heart and I know when she is praying and interceding for us. It is people like this who we need to thank God for as they are fighting in the supernatural on our behalf and on the behalf of other families. Recently she came to us after service and began to share how in the past week or so she had been seeing in the spirit as she was praying for our family, a man standing outside the circle of our family. She said he was there watching but could not get inside. At first I did not understand the meaning of that vision but as circumstances began to play out I realized the power of her prayer. Opportunity for the devil to wreak havoc was presented but because of prayer and the power of forgiveness He could not get in.

I have often explained to our teenage girls the power of soul ties. A soul tie is the knitting together of two souls that can either bring tremendous blessings in a godly relationship or tremendous destruction when made with the wrong person.

A soul tie in the Bible can be described not only by the word knit, but also by the word cleave, which means to bring close together, follow close after, be attached to someone, or adhere to one another as with glue. A negative soul-tie will hold you in bondage to a person or situation.

As a woman, it is very easy to let someone into our life who could be a negative influence in our life. We can very easily let another person touch our heart and emotions and bind ourselves to them without having any intentions of doing so. A person can actually control another through soul ties, because the minds of the two are open to one another. This is called a negative soul tie. When we are vulnerable we can open ourselves up to unhealthy relationships and create a negative soul tie. This is why I guard myself very carefully concerning relationships with the opposite sex. It is very easy to open up yourself to another person of the opposite sex if you are not being fulfilled in that area in your own relationship. This goes back to the point I made earlier about the Bible telling the husband to "love his wife even as Christ loves the church."

A young woman once shared with me her heart concerning her relationship with her husband. She knew he loved her but did not feel emotionally connected as he rarely showed affection or had intimate conversation with her. As we developed a friendship I began to see some danger signs flashing brightly before my very own eyes. She began to tell of some phone calls she had been receiving lately from an old friend, a male friend. She began talking to him for long periods of time and told me how good it made her feel. She then told me how she met him for coffee one night. Once she shared that information with me I quickly cautioned her. I told her she should never go out for coffee with someone from the opposite sex unless her husband accompanies her. It could be a very innocent meeting with no intentions of going any further but when a door is open for opportunity the devil can run with it. Most indiscretions develop from an innocent meeting at a very vulnerable time in your life. This woman was at a very vulnerable time in her life and could very easily let her guard down. When a person is not being fulfilled in their most important area of need it is easy to find others to fill it.

When I first met my husband I had quite a few male friends. I did not see any harm in having these relationships and never was cautioned by anyone concerning this. I was oblivious to the fact that this was bothering him as we were not married yet and I thought this was normal. But it was really upsetting him and I began to see these relationships through the eyes of my husband to be. I dropped all my male friendship and never looked back. And guess what? I did not lose anything but gained everything, one relationship, one soul-tie and one heart.

At times, over the years, as we dealt with some disagreement or were stubbornly holding out on each other, I would have think back to some of my old relationships and realize that I had forged soul ties that needed to be broken. The enemy would use my weak and vulnerable moments to recall another relationship or person in my life. I would wake up from a dream or thoughts that would come out of nowhere and completely throw me for a loop. As my husband and I grew in our relationship and began to understand each other's needs and worked on them, these dreams or thoughts disappeared. This showed me how powerful the soul ties are that we forge with others and the importance in maintaining healthy soul ties with our spouse. When you have a healthy soul tie with your spouse there is no need or desire for another with any other person of the opposite sex.

Now I caution our daughters on this very topic. I don't want them to have to go through what I went through or experience the same hurt and struggle I had. The lessons we learn through our negative experiences are meant to be shared so that others can learn from them and are cautioned. I don't want them or any one else to have to carry old relationships or soul ties into a new marriage and have to deal with the hurt it brings.

My husband and I believe in teaching our children about relationships from a very early age so they can prepare for that exciting journey they will face when they become of age. We hope that they will have confidence in themselves and their relationship with God before they seek someone to be joined together in marriage.

Now I want to address women concerning what God tells them in His Word. I am sure you have read this scripture many times and probably know it by heart. *"Wives submit to your own husbands as to the Lord for the husband is the head of the wife, as also Christ is head of the church and He is the Saviour of the body. Nevertheless let each one of you in particular so love his wife as himself, and let the wife see that she respects her husband."* Ephesians 5:22-23, 33

As I shared earlier, men's greatest need is to be respected and admired. As we read this scripture God is telling the wife to submit to her husband and respect him. This includes serving, honouring and edifying him. People tend to have difficulty with this passage, interpreting it as putting a woman in a very submissive position, where she has no say or input in the relationship. I see it in a very different light; I see it as a very freeing concept; we have instructions from our heavenly Father on how to understand our spouse. I now have the instructions on how to show my love to my husband. He understands and feels my love for him by the way I honour him and show my respect for who he is as a person.

As I write this chapter God has been revealing many truths to me concerning my actions and thoughts towards my husband. I want to make a difference in our relationship, that others will know where we stand as a couple and life partners. I want to let him know how much I love and appreciate him. I feel to share with you what God has put in my heart as a Pledge of Honour for my husband. I may add on to it as we continue to grow in our relationship but this is a beginning, a start of something bigger and better. This can be tweaked and changed to make it applicable to your relationship with your spouse.

MY PLEDGE OF HONOUR
I WILL NOT... ... ...

I will not belittle you, my husband, making you feel worthless and unwanted.

I will not put my chores or the children before my relationship with you.

I will not shut you out by withholding sex or refusing to talk to you.

I will not use manipulation to get you to do what I want or give me what I want.

I refuse to make fun of you or your actions in front of your family, my family or friends.

I will try my best to not involve the children in our disagreements or disputes.

I will not use them or others as leverage to get my own way.

I will not criticize your decisions or tell you I told you so when I know I was right.

I will not discount or crush your dreams before they are even birthed.

I will not allow others to tell me I have the right to leave or separate from you.

I will not hold unforgiveness as a wedge between us.

I won't let my eyes stray to something or someone that will involve a negative soul tie to form.

I will not give up on you or our marriage.

I WILL … … … … … … … … … …..

I will enjoy every moment spent with you as though it is our first.

I will love, honour and respect you for who you are as a person, the man God ordained before time to be my soul mate.

I will share with those around me how special you are and how much you have accomplished.

I will listen to your dreams and make them my own.

I will take the garbage or dung of our mistakes and use them as fertilizer for our beautiful rose garden of a relationship.

I will notice when your shoulders are a little drooped and your eyes a little tired. I will then offer a back rub, a listening ear and a caring touch.

I will be the person to encourage you, to believe in you even when no one else does.

I will send you a text, write a note or give you a call to tell you how much I love you, how much I care.

I will fight for you! If no one else will stand by you, I will. This is my choice and mission.

God has birthed this in my spirit just recently as I finished writing my list of 100 reasons. I wish I had done it sooner. I wish I could erase time and undo the mistakes of my past. My only hope or desire is to see that others do not have to wait so long. Don't let time pass you by; don't let your past mistakes or those of your spouse rule your future. Make a choice to love your wife even as yourself. Make a choice to honour and respect your husband. You will only reap what you sow and when you sow into your spouse's life you will reap blessings and joy. God's instructions on marriage were not created to separate a man from a woman but to unite them in their differences. My love for my husband has reached a new level which is indescribable to put into mere human words. It is something that transcends human expectation; it is heavenly with no earthly origin because it was given from above.

POINTS TO PONDER

- *Take time to consider your spouse and their greatest need as an individual. Is it their similarities in personality that drew you to them or their differences?*

- *Has past relationships hindered your marriage? What can you do to avoid making the same mistakes and, how can you resist negative soul ties?*

- *Plan to make your own pledge to your spouse. How would making this pledge help a relationship that is struggling to survive?*

7 Fathers and Daughters

I had first asked my husband to write this chapter for me. He is the one I have observed developing this amazing relationship between father and daughters. He is the reason I wanted to include this chapter in my book, seeing the importance of this bond formed.

But he refused, reminding me that I have been a part of this relationship as well. I have been observing all the dates, the conversations and interactions. Who would be more capable of writing about it than the woman who loves details? Yes, God has gifted women with the ability to remember details and the love to share and retell them. If you are a woman reading this book I am sure you know what I am talking about and even if you are a man reading you would surely agree with this statement.

So I am then given the honour of sharing the special moments and experiences we have learned as parents of six daughters.

When we think of the expression, "daddy's girl" we envision a little hand wrapped in the much larger and stronger hand of her father. We imagine a little girl dressed in a frilly dress, spinning in front of her father, eyes bright, smiling, laughing, and giggling behind her hand. We see the tender expression in the father's eyes as he watches his little girl twirling in front of him. This is Daddy's girl, light of his eyes, the beat of his heart, his pride and joy. It is a picture portrayed on greeting cards, magazine covers and inspirational commercials. It can touch our heart and emotions and it is a very real feeling we experience as a parent.

There is definitely a heart connection between father and daughter that is binding and strong. Even the worst of fathers will observe their daughter's desperately seeking their approval or love. The father is a role model for his daughter whether he likes it or not. Their relationship will determine what she will or will not look for in her future husband.

The father has a big responsibility to his daughter to show her the love she deserves and needs to have in order to grow and mature into a young lady. His influence will determine how she will act around other males. If the father is not meeting her need for love and acceptance she will look for love in all the wrong places. When a young girl feels secure and loved by her father she will not need to look for love. Love will meet her at the time that is right for her and when it's in Gods plan for her life.

How does a father make his daughter feel secure in his love for her? This is the big question. I believe that there is more than one way of doing this and we are going to go through each one in this chapter.

1. WORDS OF AFFIRMATION

The tongue is one of the most powerful organs in our body. It has the power to give life to a person or a situation but can equally destroy someone and their future. There are many scriptures in the Bible that describe the negative and positive attributes of the tongue. *"A wholesome tongue is a tree of life, But perverseness in it breaks the spirit."* Proverbs 15:4

The words that a father uses to speak, instruct or encourage his daughter will forge a strong bond between the two of them. The most effective words he can speak are words of affirmation. These are words that when spoken make you feel good inside. They cut through the flesh and bone and dive right into the heart. They take residence there and affirm your worth as a person and in this case a young woman's worth.

When words of affirmation are spoken from a father to a daughter it can revive a dying root and make it into a glorious tree full of health and life. When a father believes in his daughter and encourages her with affirming words she flourishes and revels in the feeling that someone truly cares for her. Someone sees her ultimate worth. Even if everyone around her seems to be against her, the fact that her father believes in her and affirms that in word and action makes her stand up strong.

Words of affirmation are important even more so to a young woman, especially when she is faced with body changes, mood swings, hormone issues and identity issues. She needs to know that despite all the changes she is going through she has someone in her life to affirm her as a person and specifically as a young lady becoming a woman. I notice it when my husband has just shared something positive and encouraging with our daughters. There is a different look upon their faces, like they have a secret they want to share. Their chin is lifted a little higher and their step is a little lighter. There is an air of confidence about them and our home grows a little more peaceful and serene. All is well for another day, another week or more until the next situation tries to shake their confidence.

This world is filled with precious and beautiful young girls struggling with their identity and finding their place in society. Each one is wonderfully unique in size, shape and personality. If all the fathers of this generation strive to invest affirming words into their daughters, can you imagine the impact? Let us encourage all the fathers we know to continually speak into their daughters' lives and form bonds that will stand the test of time.

2. TOUCH

Touch is one the most important methods of communication. It can strengthen, repair or even ruin a relationship. It is a way of expressing our feelings towards another person. Touch can bind two people together and it can break the boundaries.

Touch works hand in hand with a very large organ of our body. This wonderful organ called the skin covers the largest part of our body. It protects some of our major organs and is exposed to the outside and its influences. The skin plays a large part in sensing temperature so it also regulates the temperature of the body working in partnership with the brain. One of the most interesting and important capabilities of the skin is that it can sense pain and pleasure.

As I was researching all the different aspects of touch I was surprised to see how much benefits it has. When we look at a newborn baby, the care and love that is extended to the child through touch is by far the most soothing and comforting. It gives them a sense of security and wellbeing. When a child is left alone and is denied the stimulus of touch he or she can develop emotional or learning disorders.

Studies have shown that when we receive a gentle touch or caress our brain secretes a hormone called "oxytocin". This hormone is often referred to as the "happiness hormone". This hormone also helps create the bond between mother and child as it is released through touch. When we experience touch in the form of caring and concern we feel cherished and loved.

In relating all this information to the power of touch between a father and a daughter, we can see the significance it has. We are talking about the touch of care, a hand on the shoulder, or a gentle hug. A father is a role model for appropriate touch.

Some of us know that when we receive a hug from our spouse or a caring touch to the cheek or shoulder we feel special, loved and appreciated. Our young daughters need to experience healthy touch from someone they trust, their father. Too many young girls are searching for love and there are predators out there willing to manipulate that desire for love and use it for their benefit.

We all receive love in different ways. Some like gifts and some like affirming words or acts of kindness. But the biggest way love is received is through touch and if we can teach our young women the appropriate and pure way to be touched we have set a standard for them in their future relationships. They will not need to look outside the home for love and suddenly find themselves used and abused. They will find their ultimate worth first through their relationship with God, then through their relationships with their family, especially their father.

3. Physical presence

In the last few years my husband and I have been evaluating his time spent at home. He was working a lot of hours at several jobs, providing for a large family and was often away from the home. He was missing all the children and began resenting the fact that they would confide in me about everything in their life instead of him. We would continually discuss this issue and I had a hard time relating to his feelings. I just understood that I was home more often so it was natural that they would come to me to talk and share their day. I was not understanding his side; he was feeling left out and would at times feel like an outsider in his own home.

Too many times in our relationships we fail to see the other side of the coin. We just assume that we are right and the other person needs to understand and accept that fact. Well I began to think about how my husband was feeling. I tried to put myself in his shoes and when I did I did not feel so good. He wanted to be a part of the girls' lives as much as I did. I started to understand the importance of his physical presence in our home. When he was not there I had to be everything to everyone and fill roles that I was not fully equipped to fill. His presence was needed in the home to ensure peace and order and a sense of security. He could see or sense things in the home that needed changing or rearranging. His presence in the home was something our girls needed to feel and to see.

We have one daughter who does not like to be in the house alone. She will do anything to avoid that as it makes her very uncomfortable and nervous. Even if someone was asleep upstairs, just the fact that someone was in the house made the difference for her. She was assured that she was not alone. This is the same with the father's presence in the home. Just knowing Dad is home, he is here somewhere in the house is a comfort and strength to a young woman. Daddy's being at home, means all is well.

4. ROLE MODELLING

One of the greatest strengths of my husband I believe is his ability to be a strong role model in the home. Having six girls in the home can be enough to send a man over the edge at times. But my husband hits the issues head on and dives right into modelling for them the right way to live, the right way to make choices and the right road for education.

I remember when our oldest daughter was trying to decide what she should so for her future career. She was about 17 years old, trying to pick the appropriate courses in high school to lead her to the right university program. My husband discussed at great length the pros and cons of different career paths and encouraged her to pursue the health care field, mainly the nursing program. He was aware of the current needs in the job market and what career would be the most promising and in demand when she graduated.

I was hesitant; I saw how she struggled in science and how difficult it was for her. I am ashamed to say I could not see this career for her; I could not see how it would work out like my husband saw it. But she pursued it, studied hard, got her science marks up and is now in her last semester of a 4 year nursing program. She sacrificed her time and relationships in order to fulfill this goal. We are very proud of her achievements and her drive to succeed. I give all the credit to her and my husband who saw what she could accomplish even if some areas were weak at first.

He has been an effective role model for education. After we had four of our children and the twins were on the way, he went back to school. This was all done while he was pastoring and working a few jobs on the side. He earned two master's degrees and recently acquired his doctorate. He has often told me that one of the reasons he pursued his education is to be a role model to the children. If he could do it at his age as well as raise a family, it was possible for them to do it. He wanted to set a standard for our future generations.

Role modelling is also effective in our relationship as husband and wife. Our daughters need to see a healthy role model of their father loving and respecting their mother. It sets a standard for them in their future relationships. What our daughters see modelled in the home will either encourage them or discourage them from marriage. Many have said that young girls tend to enter into a serious relationship with a man who is just like their father. If that is true, role modelling is extremely important. Don't we all think about our children's future spouses, who they will choose and end up marrying? We do not need to worry if we are setting the standard in our own home and in our own marriage.

5. FATHER/DAUGHTER DATES

Do you remember how you felt on your first date? Were you anticipating that day with nervousness and excitement? Did it make you feel special, centered out of the crowd? Were there stars in your eyes and lightness to your step? Hopefully this was the case; first dates should be something that makes a fond memory, a positive mark in your life.

Picture a father being the first person you can experience this with. This is someone you trust, someone who respects you, someone who cares deeply for you and is considerate of your feelings. He is polite and courteous. He gives you the best he is capable of giving .There is no pressure to be someone you are not and you can speak freely about how you feel. This is an ideal date and possibly a great experience. This is what every young woman should experience for her first date.

Our daughters have been taken out on dates with their dad since they were little girls. Either individually or in a group they have experienced what it means to be treated well or to be respected, something every young woman needs and deserves to experience. Some dates may be going out to a special dinner. Some are just for an ice cream blizzard with two spoons or more. Other dates are more elaborate and incorporate bungee jumping from a giant crane out in the boonies of the great white north, or a night away for dad and daughters. It can be nachos for two or nachos for six, coffee nights or movie nights. It varies with the seasons and with the urgency of time needed to get away.

My husband regularly buys roses for the girls on their birthdays and brings it to their school. Imagine the thrill of getting called to the office to receive their roses from their dad. The special feeling of being centered out of the crowd and treated like a queen. All the other girls in the room are envious and get to observe their special relationship.

Some daughters may need a special one on one time with dad to discuss an important issue. Other times it's just for fun and relaxation, letting their guards down and enjoying each other company. Each time is important, timely and effective in meeting the needs of each daughter. Each date is expected to make memories and set standards for the young men that our daughters consider coming into their lives.

Dates with dad may seem like a strange concept in today's society but we are not of this world or governed by how society portrays relationships. We are governed by godly standards that would seek to raise our children in the ways of the Lord. When a daughter feels loved and treasured by her father she is free to be herself and confident of her identity. It creates a confident and secure woman, secure in knowing what she wants and expects in a relationship. This relationship also helps her to understand the father daughter relationship she has with her heavenly Father. This is a heavenly Father who loves and cares for her unconditionally and a Father who will never leave her or forsake her, whose promises are yes and amen.

6. ALWAYS A PRINCESS

Daddy's girl, daddy's princess is not just a term for use in fairy tales or fantasy. It is something we need to see our fathers initiating at home. It creates a feeling of exclusiveness, a picture of royalty and privilege. When this term is used it forms an image in the mind of our daughters of how special they are as young women. If they are a princess in their daddy's eye then it doesn't matter what everyone one else thinks of them. A princess symbolizes royalty, honour and respect. They have all this and more in their daddy's eyes so they don't need to look for it any where else.

The terminology or endearments we use for our children are created with the intention of earning a smile, a little giggle and an impression imprinted in their heart. Terms such as, my angel, my princess, my girlfriend are all names that create a connection between the father and daughter. She feels that she holds daddy's exclusive attention and no one else can share that privilege. It is for her and daddy alone and that in itself is enough to make her feel like a princess.

Little girls love to dress up and play princess games which includes the jewellery, the make-up and the tiara. I remember the times when our girls would get out the dress-up box which was filled with wigs, hats, jewellery, dresses, and feather bows. They would dress up to the "T", find a pair of my heels and strut around the house like the queen and princess they want to be. This is the time when I would allow them to play with my make-up soon discovering that all the colours of the rainbow would be found on their beautiful little faces. Maybe the tea set would be required and little cookies or cake to eat with the tea. Their little fingers daintily holding the china cup with tiny index fingers lifted straight up. Real princesses must dress and act the part of royalty and their great imaginations made that possible.

As they grow older they may not play the games but they still love to hear the sound of their daddy's voice calling them a princess. We are never too old to want to experience the thrill of being called a princess and most importantly, feeling like one. We all want the crown of jewels on our head and the royal treatment that goes along with it. It brings us to a place of feeling worthy, standing out in the crowd and having our moment for that day. That's why many women love to get their nails done and get their hair cut and styled. They love to go to the spa and be treated like a princess for the day.

In our Heavenly Father's eyes we are royalty because we are from a royal priesthood. *"But you are a chosen generation, a royal priesthood, a holy nation, His own special people, that you may proclaim the praises of Him who called you out of darkness into His marvelous light."* 1 Peter 2:9

The prophet Malachi prophesies about our names being written in the book of remembrance, those who fear the Lord and meditate on His name. God talks about each one of us being made into His jewels. In some translations it says He will make us his treasured possession or special treasure. *"They shall be Mine, says the Lord of hosts, On that day that I make them My jewels. And I will spare them as a man spares his own son who serves him."* Malachi 3:17

God sees each one of as a His treasure, a special possession, His jewels. This tells us that we are royalty, precious in His sight, a treasure to our heavenly Father. How much more on this earth should we see our young daughters accepting and receiving this fact not only from their heavenly Father but also from the earthly father. Our daughters are princesses here on earth and in heaven above.

Let's reinforce a sense of wonder, a sense of worth and a sense of royalty among our daughters.

POINTS TO PONDER:

- *Have you had words spoken over your life that tried to hold you back or hinder you in your relationships? Talk about how you can break the cycle for yourself and your children.*

- *How do you see "touch" to be important in your relationship with your children?*

- *What do you feel has been the most effective method of role-modeling in your home?*

- *Was there a time in your life when you felt you were treated like royalty? How did it feel? How can you make it happen now if you have never experienced it before?*

8 Not without Our children

My whole purpose of writing this book is centered on this particular chapter. I feel so strongly about this issue that I just have to write about it and pray that someone out there will listen and will learn to set priorities in their life. I have heard too many stories of broken families and broken marriages, relationships sacrificed on the altar of ministry.

I struggle with this myself as I raise our family and serve in various areas of ministry. There will always be people to minister to, there will always be various avenues to minister in, but our young ones will soon grow up and leave the home and then we wonder where time has gone. We have been entrusted with our children for such a short time while here on this earth. Precious moments are missed and opportunities to bless and invest in our children are gone in the blink of an eye.

My most favourite scripture in the Bible concerning family is found in Deuteronomy 11:18-21 *"Therefore you shall lay up these words of mine in your heart and in your soul, and bind them as a sign on your hand, and they shall be as frontlets between your eyes. You shall teach them to your children, speaking of them when you sit in your house, when you walk by the way, when you lie down, and when you rise up. You shall write them on the doorposts of your house and on your gates, that your days and the days of your children may be multiplied in the land of which the Lord swore to your fathers to give them, like the days of the heavens above the earth."*

Ministry starts first in the home. Who is going to minister in the area of forgiveness and repentance if you are not home enough to instruct and teach your family? What about Bible reading, prayer and counselling? All these need to be installed and in place so that you can then go out and minister to others. Throughout the summer when our children are off from school we incorporate daily family devotions, talk about our plans for the day and the week, discuss the chores for the day and end in family prayer.

Opportunities for questions about the scriptures read, requests for prayer and concerns of the family are presented during this time. It sets the standard for our day and allows us to minister to our family in many different ways. We pray for our family, our church and pastors, our needs and desires, and thank God daily for His blessings and mercy over our lives.

Set a standard of worship and devotion for your home and you will not regret it. It will not always run smoothly and can be definitely challenging at times. But when you hear your children ask questions about the Bible and explain how they see God working and moving you will seek no greater reward. Investing in your children takes time and effort and a lot of sacrifice. The world is continuously demanding more and more of our time and seeks to pull us away from our family units to sow disunity and destruction.

OPEN WINDOW OPPORTUNITIES

I can always tell when I have been spending too much time away from home. The peace that you have worked so hard to create in the home gradually starts to fade. It's still there yet the unrest in the home tries to overshadow it. The house begins to show signs of misuse and disarray, rules are broken and the children begin to whine and complain. Once you realize what has happened it takes a process of a few days or weeks to get everyone and everything back on track again. Your physical presence is wanted and needed to minister to the family. It is the stabilizing force for the home; our children need to see us, speak to us and feel our comfort and presence.

Maybe your teenager has just had a very difficult day, full of disappointment and confusion. They arrive home to yet another empty house. They have no one to talk to, release this stress and thoughts, so it's buried inside and an opportunity for healing and comfort is gone. Maybe that teenager begins to get used to the missing parent and stops talking completely. All this is bottled up inside and in one instant it can erupt and cause great damages.

I can definitely relate this to one of our daughters. She is generally quiet and steady and progresses by taking small but important steps. She is the type of child that will all of a sudden open up and a flood gate of thoughts, ideas and concerns will stream out. It seems to come at the most inopportune times, when I am in the middle of a project or ready to go out the door. Usually it happens when I just decided to take a quiet break away from everyone, maybe in my room alone. My flesh is telling me to say, "Can we talk later; I just began this or I need to spend time alone." But I soon realized that these moments that present themselves, though inconvenient, are "open window opportunities".

What does that mean? Open window opportunities are times we can use to listen and hear the heart of our child, spouse or even a friend. These windows of opportunity are only open for a short time and may not open again. If we are not careful we may miss them completely. Some people will let down their guards and spill their heart for a particular moment or in a particular place. But if the window closes and their heart has not been heard they may shut it for an indefinite time period. We can very easily miss that "window of opportunity."

We all have at one time or another closed the windows in our life. Maybe we have had secrets we are ashamed to share, experiences that have scarred us or loneliness that forces us to retreat behind these windows. But every once in a while the sun comes out and we want to breathe in that fresh air and change our environment. Or we tire of our solitude and throw open those windows to see who is out there to see us. We look around to see who is there, who will hear us; our heart is open and our cry is to be heard. Maybe a friend, a parent, a pastor was there at that moment and they reached out to us, helped us to open the window wider and we were heard. Most of us just want someone to hear our heart, hear our cry to be noticed, appreciated and most of all loved. Just as we have experienced these moments we must realize that our children also place themselves at times behind windows. I have learned to look for "open window opportunities" and prioritize my time according to those moments.

One way we discovered as parents that we can create an atmosphere for "open window opportunities" is through table talk. As often as we can during the week, especially Sunday, we sit as a family to eat a meal and take turns sharing about our week. When we first started it was pretty basic stuff, short answers and some reluctance to share too much information. But as it became a regular part of our week, our children began to open up more and share vital information. It amazed me to discover how much we would be missing of our children's lives if we never had these "table talks".

We began with the basics of how our week was and what was happening for the next week. Then as we progressed we started talking about the future, our goals, and our dreams as individuals and as a family. Each person had a part to play, a voice to be heard and an opinion that mattered. My husband and I were able to impart some principles about relationships, courtship and future aspirations; everyone from the youngest to the oldest participated and added value to the table. From there our children began to make lists of things like: qualities desired for their future spouse, what they want to accomplish for that year and the years ahead.

What I learned from this valuable tradition my husband started was that we were giving our children a platform to be heard, valued and appreciated. So many young people out there are crying to be heard, yet have no opportunity to do so. We busy ourselves with daily activities, work, church, ministry, and then more activities.

I like to visualize our lives at to be like the energizer bunny that keeps going and going and going... We like to think we are doing well because we are active and keep on the move. Do you remember this bunny? One thing that stood out in this picture was that the bunny was moving but had no particular destination and would twist and turn and change direction. I don't want to be like this bunny but at times I see myself following this same road. I believe that we need to switch to a different brand or type of battery. We should use the ones that need charging once in a while, where we sit down, listen, wait and pray for our children, our families our pastors. We need to recharge in God's Word, soak in His presence and use these quiet times to listen or talk with our loved ones. Your family deserves to be heard, loved and valued!

FAMILY IS THE HEARTBEAT OF MINISTRY

Our presence is physically needed at home to protect and serve the family. Ministry is a piece of the pie but the family is the foundation on which we build our ministry. It is from the platform of a good foundation that we can spread our wings and soar with confidence and strength. If the foundation is shaky then our ability to minister is deeply shaken as well.

Family is the heartbeat of ministry. It is the center core of all that you hold to be important and effective in your life. The heart is the centre of one's personality, where one's mental and moral standards lay. It contains our emotions, feelings, and desires. It is said to be the centre of our thoughts, understanding and will. In saying all this, the heart can be used as an illustration of the family and the important part it plays in our daily lives. Let's talk about the heart and its function, relating it to the family and ministry.

Your heart is a muscular organ that pumps blood to your body. It is at the center of your circulatory system. This system consists of a network of blood vessels, such as arteries, veins, and capillaries. These blood vessels carry blood to and from all areas of your body. Let us stop right here. If the family is the heart beat of ministry, it is the organ that is at the very center of your life carrying life giving product to all the different areas of your life. When the family is healthy and functioning properly it will bring health and strength to all the areas of your life including ministry. Wow! That's powerful stuff.

An electrical system controls your heart and uses electrical signals to contract the heart's walls. When the walls contract, blood is pumped into your circulatory system. Inlet and outlet valves in your heart chambers ensure that blood flows in the right direction. The heart is sent signals that allow the blood to flow properly. Is that telling you something? When we are taking care of our family, investing time and energy, love and commitment we are sending signals to "the heart" which in turn allows direction in our life. An example of this is when the heart chambers contract and ensure that the blood flows in the right direction. This is an amazing illustration. I hope you are catching it. If you think about the inlet and outlet valves in your heart, what you take in to the family unit is going to determine what comes out.

If we are not taking care of the family, the signals we send out will wreak havoc upon the health of the "heart", the family. These signals will in turn upset the direction we are taking as a family. How do you think ministry will work out for you then? We cannot ignore what's going on within our own homes and try to fix someone else's problem. Besides, we are dishonoring the gifts which God has placed in our home, throwing them aside, ignoring the issues all for the sake of "the ministry". God does not honor that. Ministry then becomes independent of God's blessings and I for one do not want to walk that road. Do you? Danger lies on each side of the pathway we walk for the Lord. If Satan can wreak havoc in your family, your children, your husband, he can definitely destroy your ministry. But if you focus on your family first, ensuring your foundation is strong and placing them in the center of your life as the very heartbeat of your ministry, you will see success in ministry.

Let's go back to our description of the heart. Your heart is vital to your health and nearly everything that goes on in your body. Your blood carries the oxygen and nutrients that your organs need to work well. A healthy heart supplies your body with the right amount of blood at the rate needed to work well. If disease or injury weakens your heart, your body's organs won't receive enough blood to work normally.

Any foreign substance that tries to invade the heart can cause a heart attack or a crippling of its functions, like somebody injecting a needle that is filled with a foreign substance. It may be harmless on its own but when it is injected into the centre of the body system it pollutes the whole body. We need to take care of the whole body and when we allow foreign or damaging people or circumstances to enter into our home, our sanctuary, it pollutes our entire family. We need to protect this heart, our home at all costs. We need to guard who or what comes into our home. If we allow someone with bad morals or habits into our home it becomes like a poison entering our blood stream and it breaks down what we worked so hard for.

There are many broken and hurt families in the church today because we forget to watch out for pollutants that seep into the cracks of our foundation. We are careful to invest time and effort for so many years, building a strong family unit. It's like going to the gym. You are eating healthy, exercising, putting time aside to train and encourage. You are building up your immune system and putting in defence mechanisms to guard the system you have worked so hard to build. When you start opening up the doors for others to enter your family you have to be very careful. They may look like they are well put together and may also give a very good first impression. If they appear to be healthy but are rotten inside, their unhealthiness will pollute your home. It's like the example of a clean, fresh and clear glass of water drawn from a spring that has been running clean and clear for many years. If you place one drip of black ink in it you will see the water slowly change and before you know it the whole glass of water has changed color. It is no longer what it used be, and it will take a lot of work and time to change the chemistry of the water to bring it back to its original state.

We need to take our time in allowing people to come into the family; they need to be a match for the home we have established. They need to be someone who is compatible and will merge with what you have worked so hard to keep. They need to be a complement to all members of your family, to keep what you have started and not sow discord. It there is any change it needs to come from the new member, not that the family has to change for them. We are taught from a very early age not to talk to or engage in conversation with a stranger. If there is a young man or woman wanting to enter a relationship with our children then they cannot be a stranger. We will never allow our children to leave the home with a stranger. This is a known fact in our home and the lines are clearly drawn.

A healthy family needs to understand and maintain principles. It should be clear what is accepted and not accepted. Our children know that if they are interested in someone then the whole family needs to get to know the person. We call it "dating the family". If there is a young man or woman interested in one of our children they need to spend time with the whole family unit. We need to see them in the home environment, interacting and sharing information with each family member. Are they kind and caring, showing interest in others? Do they carry the same values and morals you have as a family? Do they show respect to the parents and those in authority over them like their pastors or those they work for? Most importantly do they treat your son or daughter with respect and honour even above their own needs?

Our children know that if this person is not a fit for the family they do not pursue the relationship. It would not make any sense to enter into a relationship that has no future concerning the family. We have created a home that is protected from strangers; it is a strong fortress with solid walls, a refuge, a place of peace and security.

We recently experienced our first merge or expansion of the family. A young man began to show interest in our daughter. They met in college and through her witness and difference in lifestyle he began to notice her and observed that she lived for something deeper. He was invited to different church events and immediately gave his life to the Lord. He came over for Sunday dinners, engaging in family interactions, showing interest in each family member and respect for our home. He soon received baptism, growing in the Lord daily though facing much personal struggles in his own home because of his new found faith. Our daughter continued to share her growing interest in him and we went out for dinner to discuss their future together. He continued seeing our daughter through the family and in our home. We encouraged him to attend a spiritual encounter for men at our church and that same weekend he received the baptism of the Holy Spirit.

Recently he approached my husband and me to ask for her hand in marriage and we did not have to hesitate in agreeing. A few weeks later before the church body he proposed in front of more than 300 people. He with great courage and emotion shared how he wanted to ask her before the church because God is the foundation of their relationship. Our daughter with much tears and shock accepted his proposal. Many people approached us later sharing how touched they were by the proposal and how they lived out their relationship in front of the whole church family.

There was a progression of their relationship that worked with Godly principles, their great respect for each other, the family and the church.

A healthy heart, a healthy family, a healthy ministry is my heart's desire. An unhealthy heart brings disease, injury, sickness and unrest. It weakens the family. Other vital components of your life will be affected because what happens to "the heart" can be a stumbling block for those "watching" your life. Let us focus on the health of our "heart" and return to our calling as parents. It is a noble calling, though not often given enough credit.

The Bible tells us in Revelations 2: 23 that Jesus searches our minds and hearts and this tells us that He sees into our inner-most being. He too is watching our life and what we take into our heart. He cares about the heart because he knows it is the very centre of our life and from the heart streams out all the other portions of our being.

Our human heart is also the dwelling place of the Lord and the Holy Spirit. Let us allow them to live in a heart that is healthy and pure, continually being cleansed by His Spirit.

DEFINING MINISTRY

Ministry" is from the Greek word diakoneo, meaning "to serve" or douleuo, meaning "to serve as a slave." [4] In the New Testament, ministry is seen as service to God and to other people in His name. Jesus provided the pattern for Christian ministry—He came, not to receive service, but to give it.

I believe that we are all called to some type of ministry, whether it is from the pulpit or from your home. We are called to service for our Saviour and God's Word confirms this. *"Whatever you do, work at it with all your heart, as working for the Lord, not for men, since you know that you will receive an inheritance from the Lord as a reward. It is the Lord Christ you are serving"* Colossians 3:23-24

Ministry alongside the family walks a thin line. There are many checks and balances that must be applied in order for both to be healthy and successful. We will talk now about the most vital ones like protection, public eye, personal relationships and investment.

PROTECTION

The family unit must be protected at all cost. Ministry will be ongoing and could fill an entire day and evening if we allow it to. Who is the watchman of the home? Our family must not be left unprotected because we are too busy ministering to someone else's family. The man of the house must be aware of the attacks that come against the family and be on guard at all times.

In the book of Matthew it tells us that Joseph had four dreams. In the first dream the angel appeared to him and told him to not be afraid to take Mary as his wife. He had to accept God's Word and cover Mary with acceptance and protection. He must have known how much she would be talked about and even ridiculed or shunned. Yet He would protect her honor and that of his future son.

In the second dream an angel told him that he needed to take the young Child and His mother, flee to Egypt and stay there until he heard further from God. He was asked again to protect his family and in turn the future of his son's work here on earth. In his third dream he was told to return to the land of Israel and in the fourth, he was warned by God and turned into the region of Galilee. He was fulfilling the role of being the priest of the home, protecting his family and watching for their safety.

Protection is defined as the supervision or support of one that is smaller and weaker. Protection is not just from dangers of the world, it is support. The Bible tells us in 1 Peter 3:7 that *"husbands need to honour their wife as the weaker vessel"*. What is God trying to tell us about a husband's role here? I have heard it told that we need to visualize a precious, delicate vase, intricately designed, beautiful in form and function. A woman is like this vase, weak in the sense that it can easily be broken or damaged; she needs protection, and she needs support.

Who is going to make sure that this beautiful vessel is not damaged or broken? Who is going to make sure there are support systems in place to protect her from the storms of life and people that seek to destroy her? The husband who is functioning in his role as a protector will see the value this vessel holds and will treat her with kindness and respect, making sure that this vessel is well protected. Peter goes on to tell us in the same scripture, "... *as being heirs together of the grace of life, that your prayers may not be hindered"*. Man has this responsibility and if he does not fulfill this requirement his prayers can be hindered.

Why do you think God created man the way He did? From the very beginning He gave man a position of authority. It tells us in Genesis 2:15 that God took the man and put him in the Garden of Eden to tend and keep it. Then he brought all the animals to Adam to see what he would call them. God saw that there was no helper found among the animals comparable to him. God created a woman from the very depth of man, his rib taken while Adam was sleeping.

I can just picture Adam slowly waking up, stretching, and then noticing, hey something is different. Why do I feel lighter; like a part of me is missing? He could have been grasping at his stomach, maybe even counting his ribs. I can see him looking around, checking his surroundings. Maybe even looking to see if there was any new animal around, one that would help ease the loneliness he felt inside. Then he sensed the presence of his creator. Anticipation and excitement must have been coursing through his veins. The Bible tells us that God Himself brought Eve to man. He presented a gift so precious and personal only God could have thought of it.

God created the attraction a man and woman feels for each other from the very beginning of creation. We still experience that first attraction when we meet our future spouse for the first time. That was God-given; He knew just what completes us. What a wonderful and creative God we serve. The first time I met my husband there was an immediate attraction. I lost myself in those dark liquid honey eyes and that engaging smile so that my heart quickened at the very sight of him. Now being from different cultural backgrounds I tried to snuff out any feelings I had toward him. I prayed for someone tall, dark and handsome (sounds very spiritual doesn't it). This cannot be happening to me, the dark is too dark in this equation (he is from West Indian descent). Friends only, I was thinking, but that attraction kept rising to the top again. Yes, I was attracted to his deep walk with the Lord but initially, built inside of us, that attraction is there to the physical as well.

Now going back to Adam in the garden, picture him breathing a sigh of contentment as he says, "Finally bone of my bones and flesh of my flesh". Adam at that very moment decides to call her "woman" because she was taken from man. Man is now complete. He proclaims her as part of him and takes on that responsibility of protector. That is why the Bible tells us in the following verse, "*therefore a man shall leave his father and mother and be joined to his wife and they shall become one flesh."* Genesis 2:24

Man will leave his home and take on the responsibility of his wife and family. He is no longer under his parents' rule or even protection. The role has been placed on his shoulders to carry on for his new family. This is God-given, God instituted and God ordained from the very beginning of creation.

When I think of the issues we face today as families, mainly so many fatherless children, I see how we need to go back to the Word of God as our foundation. Our young men and women are growing up in homes missing the male role models and protectors of the home. Where are the fathers and why are they not taking their God given role of leading and protecting the home? There is a lack of teaching in our society today on this issue and it is wreaking havoc across the board. When the family unit is weakened and the leader of the home is taken out of the picture the devil is jumping up and down with glee. Then the roles of male and female are mixed up, reversed and called the modern family. This modern family seeps into our churches and becomes a normality in the kingdom of God.

Protection of the family and home is mandatory and ministry should never stand in the way of a man's responsibility in this area.

When we see families suffer whose parents are quite well known in ministry circles and to the secular world we question what is wrong with this picture. Ministry at all cost... at whose cost? Our families? It can't be. That is why we must consider this next point.

PUBLIC EYE

My husband and I were discussing this recently. Having a large family ourselves we discussed what would happen if our ministry were to all of a sudden be pushed to a very public stage. We realized that we were happy that this is not the case because our children are still young and we would have to install strict safety precautions for them. They would have to deal with the constant public attention and scrutiny of the media.

Talking with a pastor recently I heard some painful stories of very influential ministers struggling with family issues so ungodly that I just could not hear anymore. My heart just breaks a little each time I hear stories similar to these. How can a minister lead their flock or ministries and pretend all is well when their own families are suffering in shame and hurt? It is mind boggling to me. Don't they know that their decisions are affecting the very precious gifts of God given to them for them to protect and raise up in the ways of the Lord? What picture of God and His love does this project to their children with lives so messed up yet the message is being proclaimed from the pulpit? Is media playing too big a part of our lives today? Is it costing us our families?

One very well known minister admitted that he contributed to the demise of his marriage by putting ministry over his family. "I was so busy in the ministry, I was so caught up with the ministry, I forgot about my family," he said. "That's probably what broke the whole thing up."

He said he often preached that ministry comes first, acknowledging that he knew that teaching hurt his children. "You know what? It's wrong," he said of the teaching. "I'm here to admit I was wrong because the call of God first should touch the family. If you have no family, you can't go on anyway." [5] I am happy to say that this marriage has been restored.

The media's portrayal of the family is so distorted and twisted that it leaves us confused as to what is real. From cartoons to so called prime time "family shows", we are being exposed to mockery and disrespect, perversions and addictions, hopelessness and despair. This is called entertainment and people are sitting in front of the television soaking it all in. Role models and mentors are forged from all those hours of teaching and entertainment. If we are not careful our children will be more interested in what the world is saying. Who makes more time for them? Are you genuinely interested in what is happening in your children's world? Will they come to you and open the windows of their heart? Or, will the world speak and convince them to run in the other direction, closing more opportunities to be heard? Don't allow the world to enter your home and destroy what you have so carefully invested in.

PERSONAL RELATIONSHIPS

Another important check in balancing ministry and family is maintaining your personal relationships with your spouse and family. When a crisis occurs it can be extensive and it causes everyone to run for cover and find their own way of protection. Stress builds and it becomes all too easy to take it out on the ones closest to us. Jesus said in Matthew 12:25b "… *every city or house divided against itself will not stand.*" Walking in unity and harmony is vital to attaining victory. We need to "*put on tender mercies, kindness, humility, meekness, longsuffering; bearing one another, and forgiving one another, if anyone has a complaint against another; even as Christ forgave you, so you also must do."* Colossians 3:12-13

Our best friend should be our spouse. Whenever tension mounts due to a crisis or just the simple demands of working in the ministry we should each be quick to retreat to that place of unity and harmony. As family allies we are stronger than trying to face life on our own. Our children should feel that closeness and peace that a family home should provide. They should know that when they come home they are welcomed and accepted for who they are and know that they play a vital role in the dynamics of the family.

Our children should see us working on our relationships as well. What does that mean? Well it means they should see us talking, laughing, going out on dates, hugging, and holding hands. When they see their parents in these roles they feel safe and secure, knowing their parents are in this relationship for the long run. It helps them formulate ideals for their future mate and their goals for a happy and successful marriage.

Many of our children's friends come from unstable home environments. This could mean divorce issues, discipline problems, absentee parents, selfish ambitions and identity issues. Proper role models for our children are very hard to find today with the belief systems or lack of them in our society. The world has an abundance of role models and teachers waiting to form and instruct their young minds. If we want to raise healthy and stable God fearing children we need to be the most important persons in their lives. This takes time and lots of effort. It does not come overnight, where you wake up one morning and you are the perfect role model. If we want to be effective and inspiring role models for our children we need to model after the Lord. Our dependency on Jesus is the first step to modeling. If we can show our children that we ourselves depend on Jesus first and foremost in our life then we have taken the most important step.

The next step is to lay aside selfish ambitions. In order to be an effective role model you need to put the needs of others above yourself. Let others see you serving your husband or wife in an unselfish way, showing love and respect to the role that they play in your home. I think my husband appreciates the little courtesies I show him by making sure the house is tidy when he comes home, having a meal for him, and making sure the children are sharing vital information with him as well as myself. This also includes teaching our children to respect and honor their father as the head of the home, appreciating him for the sacrifices of time and effort put forth to support the family. That leads us to honor and respect as the next step in role modeling.

Honor and respect are key principles to model in the home. These principles are not only beneficial in the home setting but will be an effective tool for your children's role in society. If we want to make an impact in this generation we need to be modeling honor and respect so it can extend its boundaries to reach those outside our four walls. We all want to see our children succeed in this life and if we equip them with these necessary tools they can make a bigger impact than we can even think or imagine.

INVESTMENT

When we invest in our family we are investing in future ministry. While I was recently teaching in our school on the topic of *Revivalists and Reformists* we talked about a wonderful woman of God named Aimee Semple McPherson. She was constantly in the public eye in her ministry. Although she was separated from her husband, she took her children with her on the preaching circuit and invested into their young lives. Her children have shared how she took time to be with them and taught them practical life lessons and faith even though she was ministering to thousands. They never felt left out because she never allowed ministry to interfere with her time with her children. Later in her life she experienced some great stress from being in the public eye and drew back from the stage. Even then she did not stop ministering; instead, she focused on training up other pastors to carry on the work that she soon would no longer be able to do. She believed in investing in her family and in people that could carry on the faith. Her son Rolf took control over the ministry after her death in 1944. Her son led the church to expand to over 60, 000 churches today in about 144 countries. The foursquare denomination that she founded is still strong today. This is investment; this is what we all should be striving for.

When I think of the word "investment", I think of working hard at a task that you expect will give you a great return. We invest money into a house; we expect to reap a reward of more cash or equity. We invest our time into our careers, and we expect to progress and be rewarded with higher pay and longer vacations. An investment means to spend or [prepare] for future advantage or benefit, to devote morally or psychologically as to a purpose. **⁴** Can you see what I am getting at?

Investing in our children and in our spouse is vividly described and implied in the reference to a "virtuous wife" in Proverbs. This is an amazing journey of a wife and mother who describes the ideal standard or measuring rod of ministry and family.

I want to start out with expressing the value or worth of a woman striving to serve her family and the needs of her home. Proverbs tells us in 31:10,11; *"Who can find a virtuous wife? For her worth is far above rubies. The heart of her husband safely trusts her; so he will have no lack of gain"*.

Virtuous means possessing or exhibiting virtue. A virtuous person is someone of moral excellence, characterized by morality, righteousness and purity. In other words, this is a wife of valour. Wow, that is a high standard for us as women but we all need to have role models and examples to follow.

This virtuous woman has a worth that exceeds great wealth and riches. The scripture goes on to say that her husband safely trusts her. This means he is secure in his love for her and he knows she will not harm or injure him; it secures his trust in her. Now because of that security he will have "no lack of gain". I was pondering this and thinking about how this applies today. I believe he will see the family prosper spiritually, financially, physically, emotionally and mentally. That definitely is a complete package.

"She does him good and not evil all the days of her life" Proverbs 31:12. With all my heart I want to support my husband and be a major instrument in his life to help him experience all that is

good in this life. The devil would love for us to be an instrument of havoc and destruction to our spouses. Why? Because we are more vulnerable to attack as we have opened our heart to our spouse. There is an expression that says, "we hurt those we love the most," but I would love to turn that phrase around and say, "we do good to those we love the most", which actually makes more sense. We need to turn it around and realize the strength we have as a couple together. It is through our unity that our family is blessed and others around us can be impacted as well. What really struck me was the last part of this verse. It tells us that a virtuous wife will do a man good and not evil ALL the days of her life. This is commitment, this is sacrifice, this is "I am in it for the long run". This is not abandonment, not running from issues or differences; this is a life time warranty. There is no short term contract, nor escape clauses; this is the real deal, the promise of a lifetime commitment.

God could not have made it any clearer then He did in this verse. *"She seeks wool and flax, and willingly works with her hands. She is like the merchant ships; she brings her food from afar. She also rises while it is yet night, and provides food for her household and a portion for her maidservants."* Proverbs 31:13-15

We may not seek wool and flax today but we can take what is in our hands and willingly work with it. This can range from cooking, cleaning, decorating and making the home a place of peace and comfort. We can strive to shop for deals and be consistent in bringing in meals and substance into our home while avoiding debt. At times we may be up at night in order to make preparations for different events in the home or changes in schedules.

I know this may sound difficult and many may feel that only certain people are able to accomplish these feats. Well I have good news for you:

*"We can do all things through God who **strengthens** us"* Philippians 4:15

"Come to me, all you who are weary and burdened, and I will give you rest. Take my yoke upon you and learn from me, for I am gentle and humble in heart, and you will find rest for your souls. For my yoke is easy and my burden is light." Matthew 11:28-30

*"The LORD is my **strength** and my song, and he has become my salvation; this is my God, and I will praise him, my father's God, and I will exalt him."* Exodus 15:2

*"The Lord is my light and my salvation; whom shall I fear? The Lord is the **strength** of my life; of whom shall I be afraid?"* Psalm 27:1

*"O God, You are more awesome than Your holy places. The God of Israel is He who gives **strength and power** to His people. Blessed be God!"* Psalm 68:35

Yes, His strength is made available to all of us. There is not one person left out. It is with His strength that we are able to live a life of virtue and power.

"She considers a field and buys it; from her profits she plants a vineyard. She girds herself with strength, and strengthens her arms. She perceives that her merchandise is good, and her lamp does not go out by night. She stretches out her hands to the distaff, and her hand hold the spindle." Proverbs 31:16-19 .

The virtuous wife takes responsibility a little further and looks outside the home to help bring income into the family. She is industrious; she looks for ways to prosper the family, then steps out and sets herself to work.

She girds herself with strength. I remember the days when I had three children under the age of three. I would be carrying one on each hip and have one permanently attached to my leg. While this was going on I would cook, clean, wipe noses, wash and the strength of my arms never failed me. It is amazing thinking back on it now and I am fascinated when I see young moms today doing the same thing. God gives you strength for these seasons in your life that defies an explanation.

As I read this verse I did not understand the word *"distaff"* so I "googled" to find the dictionary meanings. It was interestingly a piece of wood attached to the end of a staff from which the flax or wool would be drawn in spinning by hand or by a spinning wheel. As I read a little further the dictionary had an *"Archaic"* meaning for distaff. Even this word stumped me and after some more research I discovered it is defined as meaning so extremely old as seeming to belong to an earlier period. So the archaic meaning of distaff is *"woman's work"*. There was even a side note implying that this word is sometimes offensive because it pertains to or is a characteristic of a woman. I do not find this offensive but I guess in today's society we are told that women are to rise above the archaic roles placed upon them from the beginning of time. This idea or concept has greatly crippled our marriages and own self worth as women. We sell our self short as women when we believe the lies that society has been feeding us. Women are told to separate themselves and fight for their rights as women. When this happens we lose the desire to work together in our relationships and in our home. The focus becomes self-centered and self-serving.

I believe in a woman's self worth and there should never be a time where she is used as a doormat in a relationship. But that doesn't mean that she cannot free herself in a relationship in serving, honoring, and reaching out in her home and community. I know I find freedom as a woman, mother and wife when I am doing my part to see the vision of the family fulfilled in my life.

"She extends her hands to the needy. She is not afraid of snow for her household, for all her household is clothed in scarlet. She makes tapestry for herself; her clothing is fine linen and purple. Her husband is known in the gates, when he sits among the elders of the land." Proverbs 31:20-23. She is charitable and knows that God's blessing rests on those that give to the poor. She gives with both hands meaning she gives liberally and with no reserve. Her labour is a labour of love, not selfishness. She does not just give to her own household but reaches out beyond her family unit.

When we look around our communities today we see many needs. When we serve our household we are indeed honoring God and our family but when we extend our hands out into the community we spread the blessing of God. We open our household for others to see God in us and they in turn can be blessed.

In the following verse it tells us that she is not afraid of snow for her household because her household is clothed in scarlet. I had to ponder this a little because in my mind scarlet is a rich cloth that does not imply any protection against the cold. I discovered from the Latin version that scarlet also symbolizes a "double garment". This means that her household was protected from the cold and she had no concern about them needing any protection. Scarlet and crimson were two of the firmest dyes and not easily washed out.

She wore fine linen and purple. This is a dress suitable to a queen. This tells us that she took care of herself and presented herself to her husband and household in a fine manner. When we relate this to the family today we must remember to present ourselves appropriately and take great care with our appearance. I believe we need to be attractive to our spouse by what we wear and our personal hygiene. Most of us know that men are "lookers" and they are drawn to what they see if front of them. This is why pornography is so rampant among men today. Media and businesses are aware of this and cash in on it. As a women stands in the battle for her household and her husband she can potentially avoid any conflicts by arming herself with the best that she has. We have to remember that our husbands are out there in their workplaces surrounded by beautiful women at work or in their places of recreation. I want my husband to be thinking about the wife he is coming home to at the end of the day and have great anticipation towards it rather than looking at others easily placed in his pathway and giving in to the temptation.

Proverbs 31:23 goes on to say, *"Her husband is known in the gates"*. Such a woman advances the respect in which her husband is held. Because she does such a good job of managing the household this in turn frees the man to devote himself to the interests of the community. He finds himself in a place of honour and prestige as he sits with the elders of the land. This verse has made a great impact on my life. I have experienced this principle in my walk with God. When I honour my husband and take care of my household the best way I know how, I see how it frees him to move into higher places of prominence in ministry and in the community.

I have learned and am still learning about the respect a man needs in order to be the spiritual leader in the home. If he is not respected in his own home, he loses confidence in himself and functions in a lower capacity than he is capable of. There are times I may not have agreed with some decisions made by my spouse concerning the household but as I respect him he flourishes in the knowledge that he is honored and respected. Together we find ways to make godly decisions concerning our family and ministry. Sometimes I have to bite my tongue as I see his decision was the right one and I had misjudged him or the situation. Other times I may have been correct but allowing him the final say encourages him to be more sensitive to my opinion. Either way there is nothing lost only gained.

"She makes linen garments and sells them, and supplies sashes for the merchants. Strength and honor are her clothing; she shall rejoice in time to come. She opens her mouth with wisdom, and on her tongue is the law of kindness." Proverbs 31:24-26. What an encouragement! Strength and honour are our clothing. It is the kind of strength that has power over the changes of our present circumstances.

Circumstances can easily shatter or crack a household resting on less than solid foundations. We can proudly hold our heads up high and say we have done our best, we have provided for our household. We have honoured our husbands and it is like the clothing that we wear, everyone can see it on us. It must be like a light shining before us that people can recognize. We are promised that we will rejoice in time to come. Some translations say we will "laugh" or "smile" in time to come. We look forward to the future, anticipating what it holds for us.

As we manage our households, our experiences and hard work give us knowledge and wisdom for the household and community. Wisdom is cultivated from much experience and trials; developing skills is the result. We can now encourage other young moms and those struggling in their relationships. We have been there before and can use our experiences to help others. Kindness to our household and those around us will be strength to us. Kindness is marked by good and charitable behaviour, when we have a pleasant disposition and have a concern for those other than ourselves. Kindness is also is known to be a virtue and a fruit of the spirit. A law is something binding and kindness should be a natural law, binding to our tongue.

We go on to read in Proverbs, *"She watches over the ways of her household, and does not eat the bread of idleness. Her children rise up and call her blessed; her husband also, and he praises her: "Many daughters have done well, but you excel them all."* Proverbs 31:27-29

Picture a mother hen brooding over her chicks. She watches over them, making sure they are fed, they are in order, and in her sight. She does not allow herself one idle moment because she knows the enemies that would seek to devour her chicks. We as women should be continually on guard, watching over our household. There are many influences of the world that would seek to corrupt our children our home and our relationships. We need to be continually on guard duty, watching for any signs of attack or infiltration. An idle mind is one that is open and vulnerable to attack. There may be issues that we are hesitant to confront in our home but if we allow them to slip by and not be dealt with we are just heading for bigger problems.

We need to be a role model for our household so that our family will rise up and bless us. When you have done your best in raising your children in the ways of the Lord, teaching them respect, honour and commitment then they will rise up and pay due respect to you.

When I see my children honouring God and growing in their personal relationship with God I am blessed even without them telling me because I see the fruit of what we have sown into their lives. Imagine how much more we will be blessed when they proclaim it out loud and to those around them. The Bible tells us that not only the children will call her blessed but the husband as well; he praises her.

My husband likes to tell me what a great mom I am and how he knows he's got the best. Well that's what this husband is saying in proverbs. He says there are many great women out there but hey, you know what? I got the best of the best!!!

"Charm is deceitful and beauty is passing, but a woman who fears the Lord, she shall be praised. Give her of the fruit of her hands, and let her own works praise her in the gates." Proverbs 31:30-31. This is when we get to where the rubber meets the road. Our beauty will fade, our charm can only get us so far, but our lives and working relationship with the Lord will give us the recognition and praise. All the sacrifice, all the hard work of our hands and feet, all the late night marathons, the sweat and tears, and the fervent prayers will be a distant memory compared to the blessings and joy we will receive. I look forward to the day when my master will say,

well done good and faithful servant. You have fought the good fight, run the good race and kept the good fight.

THE COVENANT

I would like to end this chapter by including our "Mungal's Covenant". This covenant was written during the time when we started noticing that there were boys coming into the picture. We were praying about how we could keep some of our family traditions and values alive. One morning when my husband was up early praying he started to write and this covenant is the result.

It is a document that our future son-in-laws and daughter-in-law will have to read and sign as a declaration of their joining their hearts and love with our family. It is also a reminder to us of our covenant as a family and our responsibility to God in honouring Him and following His commandments. You are welcome to use it and make one of your own, maybe adding your own flavour if you like. Post it in a visible place or frame it in a nice frame, hanging it in a place of prominence.

Declare to your family, friends and acquaintances your beliefs and stand as a covenant family of God. It will give you opportunity to share your faith and experience as people will ask you why you wrote it and hung it on your wall. Let it be a banner over your home and family members as a constant reminder of your covenant with God.

The Mungal's Covenant

Harrison and Kathleen Mungal *sealed August 11, 2012*

1. *I covenant to have the Word of God as the foundation of my faith.*
   1 Peter 2:6

2. *I covenant to uphold the family values and traditions which have been established. 2 Thessalonians 2:15*

3. *I covenant to be honest and faithful to uphold my integrity as part of this family. Proverbs 10:9, Psalms 25:21*

4. *I covenant to protect this family in doing that which is good, right and true.*
   2 Chronicles 31:20-21

5. *I covenant to honour my father and mother, and maintain a close relationship with each family member. Matthew 15:4*

6. *I covenant to receive the blessings of God upon my life.*
   Psalms 115:14-15

7. *I covenant to be a reflective image of God following the example of Jesus Christ, laying a foundation of prayer and fellowship with the Holy Spirit.*
   Colossians 1:15-17, 2 Corinthians 3:18, Hebrews 1:3-4

8. *For this God, our God is forever and ever. He will be our guide, even to death. Psalms 48:14*

POINTS TO PONDER:

- *Have you missed out on some "open window" moments with your children? It is not too late, you can begin today and watch and pray for opportunities to listen and speak into their lives. What can you do to encourage such moments to happen?*

- *How have you handled new people from the outside coming into your family circle? Have you compromised for them or have they had to work on fitting into your family?*

- *Do you believe that God ultimately created the attraction that man and woman have for each other? What does that say to us about our relationships?*

- *Does the Proverbs 31 woman intimidate you? Or can you break down each verse and see how it can apply to your life, one step at a time? What has been the hardest aspect of her example for you to follow?*

9 RESPONSIBILITIES & REWARDS

I want to share with you something very precious and meaningful that God began to reveal to me for each of our children. Remember I shared with you some of our experiences in the mission field and how my relationship with God began to develop on a very personal level. Well, it was during this time that God gave me one word for each child and what this meant to me. As each child grew and our family expanded I started understanding the significance of each word and the promise attached to it. I want to share with you this experience. I hope this will be an encouragement to you and help you understand this awesome responsibility we have been given of parenting our children.

Karleen, our first born, bright-eyes, curly hair, and infectious laughter, strong-willed to the bone. God gave me the word "**delight**" for you. Yes I can understand in the natural realm the implications of this word. Being the oldest and first of our children you have set the standard and raised the bar for the rest to follow. We delight in all the first steps, first words, first tooth, first bike ride, first swim, first to go to school, first to succeed in your studies, first to enter puberty, cry, plead, and suddenly attract much attention from the opposite sex. But through it all you held your faith; you faced challenges, not perfectly but strong for a young woman. We delight in all that we see you grow in and all that you have accomplished so far, with much expectation for a great future. You are a delight in our eyes and we marvel at this wonderful creation that God has entrusted into our care.

When you come home from a busy day of working hard, saving for your education, and come and hug me saying, "Mommy, I'm tired", I just melt and allow that moment to linger. You are so independent yet so tender and loving, reaching out to pull at the strings of my heart. You are our "delight". As much as this means to us, you have been given this word to me from God himself. And because it comes from Him it has much more meaning than we can understand in the natural realm. It comes from heaven itself.

The scripture tells us in Psalm 37:3-4; *"Trust in the Lord, and do good; dwell in the land, and feed on His faithfulness. **Delight** yourself also in the Lord, and He shall give you the desires of your heart."*

As much as you are a delight to us you are to delight in Him. So much so that He promises you that if you delight in Him, He will give you the desires of your heart. The heart encompasses both the physical organ and a person's inner yearnings. God sees right through to your heart and can sort out and analyze what lies within your heart. He knows you down to your deepest core and can answer your heart's cry. Allow Him to search your heart and delight in the Lord who cares enough to promise to answer your heart's cry!!

Psalm 37:23-24; *"The steps of a good man are ordered by the Lord, and He **delights** in his way. Though he falls, he shall not be utterly cast down: for the Lord upholds him with His hand."* This is a promise from a faithful God, who delights in seeing His child walking in the pathway that He has ordained for you. God has ordered your steps and all you have to do is walk in them. This takes complete trust and faith. He will uphold you with His hand. This is the same hand that formed you in your mother's womb. This hand has continually guided you that though you may fall you will not be defeated or destroyed because God upholds you and that is His promise to you. Continue to delight in your God!

Jeremiah 9:23-24; *"Thus says the Lord: Let not the wise man glory in his wisdom, let not the mighty man glory in his might, nor the rich man glory in his riches; but let him who glories glory in this, that he understands and knows Me, that I am the Lord, exercising loving-kindness, judgment, and righteousness in the earth. For in these I **delight**, says the Lord."* Let this be your goal, to know God! Allow this scripture to teach you to define your life and service by your desire to know God. For God delights in this; He wants you to glory in the understanding and knowledge of Him.

Kristan, second in line, quiet, serene, beautiful; you are like the calm after a storm. God gave me the word "**peace**" for you. You came into the world feet first, fighting against the odds and an answer to the prayer spoken over you as you struggled to make your entrance into this world. Your dad laid his hands over my womb and rebuked the devourer, taking authority over the situation in Jesus' name. Yes, you are our miracle, a gift of peace. When you came home from the hospital we could not understand why you were so quiet, so peaceful, and so serene.

I remember when you had a fever at a few weeks old and you were crying a lot which was very unusual for you. Your dad and I prayed for you and immediately you stopped crying and fell asleep, fever gone. You were so young and yet I believe you were touched by the Holy Spirit's power. That was just the beginning of the many miracles God would do throughout your life. When you were just maybe about three years old, you woke up from your nap to tell me that Jesus came into your room, kissed you and told you that he was coming back soon. You were so excited about this that when your dad came back late at night you immediately ran to him to share the same news. Jesus came in your room honey; He talked to you and you have not forgotten, have you?

You have found that many a person have come to you with their issues and problems, crying, frustrated and wanting to be heard. You often have wondered why they come to you. It's the peace that flows through you, the calmness, the quietness and strength in it. Even when I have had a rough day you have a way of focusing and diffusing the difficulty of the day, helping me to realize it's not that big of a deal. You are our peace!

Psalm 37:37, "*Mark the blameless man, and observe the upright; for the future of that man is **peace**"*

Isaiah 26:3, "*You will keep him in perfect **peace**, Whose mind is stayed on You, Because he trusts in You.*" As you face the challenges of life keep your focus on Jesus and He promises to give you perfect peace. So even if everything around you is in turmoil you shall have peace, and not just peace but perfect peace, a peace that passes all understanding because it comes from above. Isaiah 55:12, *"For you shall go out with joy, And be led out with **peace**; The mountains and the hills Shall break forth into singing before you, And all the trees of the field shall clap their hands."*

John 14:27, *"**Peace** I leave with you, My **peace** I give to you; not as the world gives do I give to you. Let not your heart be troubled, neither let it be afraid."* God gives you a peace that no person or worldly possession can ever give to you. He says that it is "MY PEACE"; this is a special gift from God to you. The world's peace may last for a moment or a day but God's peace is everlasting and eternal. This peace keeps our heart from being troubled or afraid. When you continue to grasp that truth you will extend that peace to others as well.

There are many more scriptures to share but I will leave you with this one. Philippians 4:6-7, *"Be anxious for nothing, but in everything by prayer and supplication, with thanksgiving, let your requests be made known to God; and the **peace** of God, which surpasses all understanding, will guard your hearts and minds through Christ Jesus."*

Kanesha, our third daughter is bubbly, fun-loving and persistent. You are beautiful, inside and out. God gave me the word "joy" for you. You have such a joyful spirit, and have touched my heart many times because of this. As a young child growing up in the mission field you were loved and sought after by the people of that country for the delight you brought to them. As you are growing into a young woman you have experienced changes in your life that would try to extinguish that joy. There were times when I would cry out to God asking Him where my Kanesha disappeared to and who was this stranger in my home. But God reminded me of the word "joy" and to proclaim it over your life. So I have and daily thank God for His gift of "joy" to us.

I love the sparkle in your eyes and your hearty laughter which continues to be contagious to those around you. Not only are you this but so much more. You are persistent in your faith and in your health. You have a determination to achieve and excel in these areas and inspire those around you to do the same. Psalm 5:11, *"But let all those rejoice who put their trust in You; Let them ever shout for **joy**, because You defend them; Let those also who love Your name Be **joyful** in You."*

You are a joy to behold as a young woman and a testimony to the faithfulness of God. Let that joy bubble over and be your strength. When we trust in God and see Him defeat our enemies we need to rejoice and shout for joy. The love of just His name alone should bring joy to our spirit.

Psalm 16:11, *"You will show me the path of life; In Your presence is fullness of **joy**; At Your right hand are pleasures forevermore."* God will continue to direct your path and we are promised that just His presence alone in our life is fullness of joy. Let that be strength to you; His presence alone can fill you with His joy. Habakkuk 3:18, *"Yet I will rejoice in the Lord, I will **joy** in the God of my salvation."*

John 15:11, *"These things I have spoken to you, that My **joy** may remain in you, and that your **joy** may be full."* Remember that we cannot rely on the temporal joy that this world may give us. For it will soon leave and make you feel empty inside. But God promises us that "MY JOY" may remain in you that YOUR JOY may be full. His joy is not temporal but eternal and even if the world is falling apart around you His joy will remain in you and will be full. This scripture has helped me so much in my own walk. Knowing that the Joy of Jesus resides in me and I can draw from it at any time and in any situation is helpful. It is a strength to me and can be a strength to you as Nehemiah 8: 10 tells us that the joy of the Lord is our strength. Acts 2:28, *"You have made known to me the ways of life; You will make me full of **joy** in Your presence."*

3 John 1:4, *"I have no greater **joy** than to hear that my children walk in truth."*

This is such a powerful and "on the mark" statement. Your dad and I have the greatest joy when we see you walking in the truth of God and living a life pleasing to Him. You are one of the greatest gifts we have received from our heavenly Father and we rejoice in His mercy and grace to bestow such a gift to us.

Kyra, our fourth daughter, is vivacious, affectionate, engaging and beloved. Before you were born God spoke to your dad regarding your birth and your name. We were living in Croatia at the time and we were looking for a place for you to be born. The hospitals were too expensive for foreigners and the locals were even encouraging us not to use their hospitals. We tried the United Nation base that was situated in Split during the war and even they were resistant for us to use their hospitals. Our last resort was to buy a ticket for Toronto and for me to stay by my parents until you were born. While I was in Canada Dad stayed in Croatia with Karleen and Kristan and it was a difficult time for him. During this time God spoke to Dad and told him why he was having another girl and He gave the name "Kyra" and the Croatian name "Danica". He did not know what the Croatian name meant until one of our church members told us. Danica means "the bright and morning star". You have continued to be a bright shining light in our lives.

God gave me the word "**love**" for you. From the very start, as soon as your little arms could reach around our neck you were showing your affection toward us. You love to show affection and are very sensitive to those around you. A sharp word would start the flow of tears from those large brown eyes and wound your tender heart. We won't mention the childhood nickname earned from those big tears.

You come up behind me and still wrap those arms around me holding on till I weakly protest. But your love is big and contagious as well. I often wonder how you can smile continuously and not get sore cheeks. It is quite amazing and I haven't figured it out yet. Love is what you give out and yet you absorb it like a sponge from your loved ones.

Psalm 91:14, "*Because he has set his **love** upon Me, therefore I will deliver him; I will set him on high, because he has known My name.*" God is telling you that when you set your love upon Him then He will deliver you and set you on high. What a privilege and honor that He will bestow upon you if you just love Him with all of your big heart. Keep focusing that love in the right direction; let God fill the empty places of your heart so that the love you want to pour out will be from a pure source.

Matthew 5:44,45, "*But I say to you, **love** your enemies, bless those who curse you, do good to those who hate you, and pray for those who spitefully use you and persecute you, that you may be sons of your Father in heaven; for He makes His sun rise on the evil and on the good, and sends rain on the just and the unjust.*" God calls us to love those who hurt us the most, those who may curse you or use you for their own means. Why would He ask you to love such people? You must love them because you are a daughter of your Father in heaven.

You are a representative of your Father here on earth; what you say or do is a reflection of the one who raised you. If you want to be a daughter of the most High King, you need to love like He does, unconditionally. John 14:21, *"He who has My commandments and keeps them, it is he who **loves** Me. And he who **loves** Me will be **loved** by My Father, and I will **love** him and manifest myself to him."*

Lastly, I will share this scripture with you. John 12,13, *"this is My commandment, that you **love** one another as I have **loved** you Greater **love** has no one than this, than to lay down one's life for his friends."* If you want to experience the fullness of God in your life where He will show Himself to you, you will need to keep His commandments. Your faithfulness to His Word as you study and apply the Word in your life shows God that you love Him. It is an expression of love that guarantees His love, the love of the Father and the Son.

Jadon and Jayonna, our twins, an unexpected gift, an example of the goodness of our God and how He loves to surprise us with good and perfect gifts. God gave me the two words "double portion" definitely a biblical term and has great spiritual significance. What can I say about you both?

Well **Jadon**, you arrived three minutes earlier than your sister. You are our first son, our only son until our son-in-laws arrive on the scene. You are an inquisitive and sensitive boy. Your teachers always make comments concerning your observations and consistency in bringing out points no one else would notice. Not only are you unique in your observations but you are sensitive to the needs of others. You would be the one to notice if I was tired or something was bothering me. You will sneak a hug and ask, "Mom how was your day? Are you ok?" Then would ask, "Is there anything I can do for you?" You are polite and appreciative of what you have and what people do for you. You are our "double portion".

Jadon is a Hebrew name meaning **"thankful"** or "he will judge". Your name appears in the Old Testament as the name of one of the builders of the wall of Jerusalem. *"And next to them Melatiah the Gibeonite, Jadon the Meronothite, the men of Gibeon and Mizpah, repaired the residence of the governor of the region beyond the River."* Nehemiah 3:7

I see that your name was chosen well because I know that you have a very thankful spirit and mind to those around you. We are also very thankful for having our first son after five girls. You are an answer to a prayer spoken many years before you were born. Sometimes we do not understand the reasoning as to why our prayers are not answered as quickly as we would like them to be. However, God in his ultimate wisdom and care brought you into our lives at this moment with your twin sister. We are truly thankful in all sense of the word.

This word "thankful" describes your personality and your caring toward others. Another word for thankful is appreciative, as you show your thanks in simple words and acts, it will touch the lives of people in your pathway. *"Enter into His gates with **thanksgiving**,*

*and His courts with praise. Be **thankful** to Him, and bless His name."*
Psalm 100:4

A thankful heart is required in our worship of the Lord. We will enter into his courts when we come with a thankful heart filled with thanksgiving. *"Giving **thanks** always for all things to God the Father in the name of our Lord Jesus Christ." Ephesians 5:20*

*"Be anxious for nothing, but in everything by prayer and supplication, with **thanksgiving,** let your requests be made known to God." Philippians 4:6.* A thankful heart will also free us from worry and anxiety. It will put us in the right place to bring our requests unto God. It also allows us the freedom to pray freely and without a second thought, knowing that it rests in God's hands to bring forth the answer.

According to the Jewish historian, Flavius Josephus, Jadon is the name of a minor prophet in his writing on the "Antiquities of the Jews." [4] So you see that your name has much meaning biblically and for you personally. I believe you will be a builder of people, building up their confidence and inspiring others to reach their highest potential. You will speak also for God, like the prophets of old, where you will be able to share God's heart to the lost and the backslidden. A double portion of this you will have, like your twin sister so that you can reach those others cannot reach.

Jayonna, our little go-getter, you came into this world with a weight under five pounds. Yet you soon caught up to your brother, eating while he would sleep, a feisty, energetic little one. You soon would prove to be the persistent one, never backing down from a challenge, keeping up to your brother was no problem for you and always helping out with your younger sister and teaching her at every opportunity. You have been such a blessing to us.

Every night you have taken the role of reading the Bible out loud to your younger sister. To see you doing this on your own and with such faithfulness is astounding. You continue to do acts of kindness around the home and for your siblings. I have asked your sisters and brother what they see in you and they agree on the word **kindness**.

Kindness is the act or state of being kind and this is shown by good and charitable behaviour. It also means that you have a pleasant disposition and a concern for others. Kindness is also a virtue. It is said that kindness does not just benefit the giver but it releases neurotransmitters that make you feel content and relaxed. It is healthy to be kind! As God gave me the word for "double portion" for you and Jadon, so I believe you have received a double portion of kindness upon your life. "*And be **kind** to one another, tenderhearted, forgiving one another, even as God in Christ forgave you.*" Ephesians 4:32

God in His Word commanded us to be kind and forgiving because God Himself is forgiving and forgave us. As you act in **kindness** and from a tender heart, you are acting as God Himself would.

"*But love your enemies, do good, and lend, hoping for nothing in return; and your reward will be great, and you will be sons of the Most High. For He is **kind** to the unthankful and evil.*" Luke 6:35 Even our enemies need to be shown kindness. God's kindness is not limited but extended to all. Remember that the kindness that we extend should not be done for favors or for things in return. We must act from our heart and know that our reward is not dependent on people but on God. He is our rewarder and He says that your reward will be great.

We have a great example of a virtuous woman in the book of Proverbs. As you are a young woman of God you too can be this woman who opens her mouth with wisdom. When you speak with wisdom there is always an action incorporated with it and that is the act of kindness. Our love and kindness is extended not only by the words we speak but by our actions and deeds. *"She opens her mouth with wisdom, and on her tongue is the law of **kindness**." Proverbs 31:26*

The Bible tells us in Luke 5:17-26 the story of the paralyzed man who desired to be healed by Jesus. His friends carried to him to the house where Jesus was but there was a great crowd and they could not get through. These four very determined friends climbed the roof with the paralyzed man on the cot, something very difficult to do and lowered him through the roof, directly in front of Jesus. What a way to get Jesus' attention. But it worked and they had Jesus' full attention. Jesus saw their faith and he healed the man. The action of this man's friends placed him directly in Jesus' path. If they had not acted in kindness, and pushed through, he may have never seen Jesus. When the man rose up, completely healed he gave glory to God.

Remember Jayonna that your kindness may not always be noticed by man but God will get the glory and that is the most important part of your gift. We look forward to seeing what you will accomplish as you grow into a young lady.

Janelle, you were a wonderful surprise; we cannot imagine our family without you. God gave me the word **"grace"** for you. You are God's gift of His grace extended to us. It is by His grace that He gave you to us and by His grace we look forward to seeing God's plan revealed through you. You are a happy, fun-loving, cute as a button little girl who wins peoples heart by your giggles! Our youngest, you enjoy being the "baby" and "daddy's girlfriend". You love to dance and dress-up, filling the room with your energy and exuberance for life. Your curls bouncing as you prance around with laughter and mischief.

Who can forget our "tea for two" tea parties together on the front porch with crackers and cheese, or the secret videos you would send to me on my phone making up your own love song to me! Treasured moments, and precious time spent together.

"Grace" derives from the Greek, *charis*. In secular Greek, *charis* was related to *chairo*, "to rejoice." It denoted "sweetness" or "attractiveness." [4] There is an attraction to you as a person and the sweetness goes right along with it. It came to signify "favor," "goodwill," and "loving-kindness". God has indeed favoured us as parents and bestowed on us this wonderful gift. When I think that we almost planned to stop at having six children, I then remind myself and thank God for his loving-kindness shown through you, Janelle.

In the New Testament, "grace" (156 times) takes on a special redemptive sense in which God makes available His favor on behalf of sinners, who actually do not deserve it. Grace is such a special word because it entitles us to His unlimited favor even though none of us deserve it.

Esther 2:16-17 *"And when Esther was taken to King Ahasuerus, into his royal palace, in the tenth month, which is the month of Tebeth, in the seventh year of his reign, the king loved Esther more than all the women, and she won* **grace** *and favor in his sight more than all the virgins, so that he set the royal crown on her head and made her queen instead of Vashti."* God used Esther in a great and mighty way. He had a special plan for her life just like He has for you. It was grace and favour that won the heart of the king. You have the capability to capture the attention of the world through this grace. As long as your focus is on glorifying your Saviour the grace that has been given you will bring you into places and situations others may never be able to experience. Guard your heart and mind and He will show you things you never dreamed or imagined were possible.

It tells us in Corinthians 12:8-9 *"Three times I pleaded with the Lord about this, that it should leave me. But he said to me, "My* **grace** *is sufficient for you, for my power is made perfect in weakness." Therefore I will boast all the more gladly of my weaknesses, so that the power of Christ may rest upon me."* Know that His grace is available to us even though we have done nothing to deserve it. Never take for granted the sacrifice that was made for you. For it is in our weakness that He makes us strong and gives us the power to overcome.

This is just a part of what God has given me for each child. There is so much more to write and so much more to say that I could fill this whole book. But my purpose was to give you a peek into our family and help you to see the bigger picture for your own family. Seek God concerning the purposes and plans He has for each one of your children or if you do not have children, the purposes He has for you as a couple.

God speaks and we just need to listen for His voice. He cares about every part of our life and desires to speak into our relationships. God has created each intricate part of us. We have the responsibility to see that each part is working properly and to its best potential. When we do this we will see the reward. It may not be the next hour, or day or even year but we are promised a reward for our efforts. What we sow into our family and our relationships **WILL** bring forth a harvest.

Points to Ponder

- *Has God given you certain words, dreams or visions for your children or your spouse? What have you done about it? If you have never thought about this before or never asked God for this, think about asking for it today.*

- *Why do you think it is important to know the plans and purposes God has for your family?*

- *What rewards have you seen from what you have sown into your family and relationships? Are you praying for more fruit and more harvest for your family?*

10 COUNTING THE COST

"For which of you, intending to build a tower, does not sit down first and count the cost, whether he has enough to finish." Luke 14:28

My husband and I discussed our family plans early on in our relationship and knew that a large family was something we both desired. I was happy to hear that he wanted the same and we began to plan without much thought to the cost of raising a large family. We soon learned how to economize in order to provide for our growing family. We were focusing on providing for our family's physical needs and worked hard at making sure they were cared for.

Ministry in the early years was lean years and financially we had to watch every penny that came our way. I remember doing our first cross country preaching tour across Canada with two small children and being a few months pregnant. We would stay in people's homes for the most but at times had to find our own accommodations with a limited budget. Some of these rooms were so dirty we would sleep on top of the covers and grit our teeth as we heard little creatures running around the room at night. I don't have very fond memories of these hotel rooms and the squalor we found there but it makes me appreciate what we have today.

With every building project you have surprise costs that may occur at the most inconvenient times. One such example was during our time as missionaries in Croatia. We struggled with finding a home to live in and because of our faith and the war going on at that time people did not trust us. Anything that was different than their faith was considered a "sect" or "cult". We arrived in Croatia with little more than a few suitcases, three small children and big dreams. We did not know the language or anyone living there. The missionaries who were there before us ushered us into their apartment and left the next day. We were left alone, a young couple beginning a new venture in a war-town country. This apartment we found ourselves living in was very expensive and had a mould problem so we eagerly began seeking another place to live.

We finally found another apartment above the new landlord and had use of a very small yard with a fig tree and some very nice orange trees. The girls loved it there and would play in the small yard picking some of its sweet fruit. I did not care for the messy figs that kept falling onto the cement walkway that needed cleaning each day. Or the fact that I didn't have a washing machine and had to wash everything in the bathtub (I never complain about laundry anymore). But the girls were happy and the place was clean. We also had a young Croatian man living with us as our interpreter and dear friend. He was a close friend of my husband and like a brother to me.

One evening we heard a very loud and persistent banging on our door. It was the owner of the apartment and he was very angry, yelling and demanding that we open the door. Our interpreter opened the door and the owner grabbed him by the collar and was dragging him out the door. He demanded that we leave right away because we were not Catholic and he did not want us in his home. Needless to say we were very frightened and the girls very upset. We had to leave that night without a clue where we would go. We decided to call one of our church members who lived alone with her son outside the city. She graciously took our family of five in and our interpreter at the risk of being found out by her landlord. We slept in her living room for almost a month until another home was found for us far outside the city.

After we settled in our new place we would ride the bus back and forth to the city with our small children taking at least an hour each way. We were thankful for a new home that was clean and appropriate for our family. I often would become lonely so far away as I did not go with my husband to the city each day. I would remain home with the children but during those times I grew closer to my Lord and Saviour as only He could fill the loneliness I felt inside. My husband would go everyday into the city to evangelize in the city centre. So many young people filled the city as work was scarce and a war was raging outside the city. There was a spirit of hopelessness and despair, and only Jesus could bring hope back to their hearts. My husband soon earned the nickname "the best pope in town". He would spend time with them, listening, laughing and sharing the gospel. It was something he enjoyed immensely but often would be concerned about the drug problem among the young men. He began to work among them and earn their trust; soon we began to see young people come into the church one by one. It was a very slow process as there was a lot of suspicion and distrust especially among the parents of these teenagers.

One incident that will never leave my mind occurred during this time. It concerns a young man who was new to the faith and growing in his walk with God. His face would glow with the presence of the Holy Spirit and he would carry his Bible everywhere he went even bringing it home with him. His parents did not like this and his growing faith so they gave him an ultimatum - this Jesus, or us. This brave and dedicated young man chose Jesus and for the first few nights slept by the beach having no place to stay. When we found out we brought him into our own home. He only stayed a few days before God opened a huge door for him. He got a job that included a small flat and meals. This is quite amazing since jobs were so scarce and the country was in the middle of great crisis. God really showed himself to this young man and to us as missionaries. We had seen God move continuously during our two years in Croatia. Though the persecution was great the miracles and wonders were greater.

During the more difficult times when the heaviness of the spiritual atmosphere was very thick and heavy like a weight on our shoulders, we would take a boat to a small island off the coast of Split. It was a time to get away and reflect and also to pray for the city. My husband would take a group there to spend the night praying by the beach. On one occasion a young woman who had been attending the church brought along two of her friends from her town outside of the city. They were doing their time in the army as all young men do when they reach a certain age, so they came in their army clothes to the prayer meeting on the island. To their surprise as the young group began to pray they saw fire on top of their heads. The young lady showed them how this was in the Bible, when on the day of Pentecost the Holy Spirit appeared as tongues of fire. No doubt this was a big factor in them giving their heart to the Lord.

We eventually moved back to the city when we found an apartment suitable and landlords that actually trusted us. The family had moved out of the city in a country home and needed to rent out their apartment in the city. We developed a good relationship with them and had some wonderful conversations concerning God and faith. This apartment was on the ninth floor of maybe at least 15 or more floors. This was not a big issue for me except that the very old cage of an elevator broke down often. More times then I can count I would climb those flights of stairs with three small children and a stroller. Thank God for the strength given at those times. One time we were riding the elevator up to the apartment when it broke down between floors and out went the lights. It was several hours before we had someone come and get us out. I never complained about climbing all those stairs again!

Unexpected circumstances, obstacles in our pathway, and unplanned surprises may come our way periodically. We can carefully make plans for our future and our family but it does not always flow the way we want to or expect. We have to trust God to bring us through those times and allow these circumstances to strengthen us and our dependence on God. One thing my older girls tell me is that they never have any bad feelings or remember bad experiences connected with our lean years. I think the main reason is the positive attitude we have had through it all and our focus on family time. They remember the simple pleasures of an outing or cost free excursions found through out the community. The focus was not on the cost or expensive material things or activities but the time spent together.

Community events, summer festivals, bank openings, library workshops and contests are all great ways to spend quality family time together without spending a lot of money. Today many families believe that the more expensive the gift or excursion the happier they will make their children. We believe that the time spent together is more important than having the latest gadget or toy. Children desire to have their parent's undivided attention even if for just a few hours a day. I think the biggest sacrifice that we can make is our time, our time given only for our children or spouse.

My husband will often surf the net looking for deals on hotels to spend a night away with the family. He finds amazing deals and can take the entire family away for the night at a very little cost. One time he booked a hotel room that was only 20 minutes from our house but was attached to the Toronto International Airport. It was pretty awesome to see the planes take off and land from our hotel room and it was a time away from our regular day to day lives.

It is said that we should count the cost but make the sacrifice without regret. What does that mean to you? To me it means that every sacrifice we make for our children and family should never be looked back upon with regret. When we sacrifice we are giving up something to benefit another. Our sacrifices should not be spoken about in a negative way or in a way to bring guilt or regret to another. We need not look back on the decisions or choices we have made concerning our children. We should look ahead toward progress and positive changes. I have heard of parents who tell their children regularly of all the sacrifices that they have made for them in order for their children to feel guilty for their behaviour or ingratitude. If we were to do this we will only be pouring guilt upon them and make them feel unworthy of our love.

Let me share a short story with you. A young couple deeply in love with great hopes and dreams for the future began planning for the arrival of their first child. The baby girl soon entered the world all pink and rosy, exhibiting a sweet temperament, and bright blue eyes. Everyone that came to visit remarked on how beautiful she was and how much potential she had for the future with such a sweet spirit. Her parents were blissfully happy and smitten with her. They named her Annie after her grandmother and they began to make plans for her future. Maybe she will grow up to be a doctor, a lawyer or maybe a famous ballet dancer. She showed much promise of these things as she excelled in her studies and in the arts.

Her parents worked hard to support her in all her extra activities, working long hours and overtime. Annie began to find herself home alone many days and evenings. She would come home and find no one to share her day with, her triumphs and her failures, her disappointments and her successes. She began to look for someone or something to fill the emptiness she felt inside. Her grades dropped, her lessons skipped and new interests formed with people that had time for her. Her mother and father approached her the day her report card came home. They were shocked at what was happening to their little girl. Hadn't they worked very hard to give her everything she wanted? They fought long and hard, each having a reason for their stand. No one backed down or apologized. Annie's parents reasoned that they had done everything they could to guarantee that she had everything she needed. Without realizing it they added to her disappointment by verbalizing their sacrifice for her, asking her why wasn't she grateful.

That evening Annie left the home, weeping and defeated. She felt misunderstood and alone. Who was listening to her? Who cared about what she thought? Why did she now feel this guilt upon her of her parents sacrifice to provide for her financially? What was wrong with her? She never felt as alone as she felt that moment.

She found a temporary place to stay with a school friend. Her parents began to pray and seek counsel concerning their daughter. They talked to some other couples in their home group who had experienced something similar with their child. As they began to seek answers they realized that they played a big part in her situation. They asked their home group to pray and found that their new curriculum for the next few weeks was on the family unit. Together they poured over scripture and examples from their lessons on the family. During one their studies they came across a statement that hit them hard and true. It said that we must count the cost but make the sacrifice without regret. They realized that they truly did not count the cost of the type of sacrifice they made for Annie. The cost of their time and money did not matter as much as they thought it would. Their commitment to her as parents mattered so much more. Where had all the time gone? They spent all the days and nights working for something they thought was right, but it was actually destroying their relationship with their daughter. Their sacrifice was made with regret because it was the wrong choice.

They began to slowly realize that their time and doing without some of the extra activities and money would have been the better sacrifice to make for their daughter. They prayed and fasted for their daughter and repented of the wrong choice they had made. Eventually their daughter returned home. Annie began to see the changes in their house as her parents made time to be home, eat together, communicate more and just learn to have fun together as a family. Her grades went up and she picked one activity to excel in where her whole family could attend and be involved in. They made some sacrifices financially but soon realized they didn't really need all the extras they thought they needed.

We must count the cost but make the sacrifice without regret. We should not rehash every price we have paid to make the way straight for our children. As guardians and inheritors of the wonderful gift of our children God has entrusted to us, we need to remember that God has counted us worthy of the high calling of parenting them. Never allow regret to poison the future of your family.

POINTS TO PONDER:

- *What can you do that will provide some quality time with your children that is inexpensive but fun?*

- *Have you ever considered the fact that you can make sacrifices without regret? How would that make a difference in your family dynamics?*

- *Remember that though we may experience difficult times financially and emotionally we can face them with a positive attitude that will help our children to have no regret concerning their upbringing. Count the cost but make the sacrifice without regret!*

11 THE MYTH FACTOR

What is a myth? It is generally said to be an invented story, idea or concept. It also can be an unproved or false collective belief that is used to justify a social institution. We are challenged and tested daily with myths about the family and women. These myths are coming from the community we live in and even our church today. Sadly to say these myths are believed and practised without any proof or searching into if they are really true or not. We pass on beliefs and assumptions without a thought to whether they are fact or fiction. I believe some of it is just laziness on our part. It's like a parent telling you to do something for them or obey them just because "I said so". You are given no reasoning and no explanation and you just act because your parents said so.

Let me give you an example. I live in the wonderful country of Canada. Now someone who does not live in Canada and has never visited our beautiful country may assume to know about my homeland. They can look at the pictures and talk to others about the various things Canada has to offer and the wonderful weather we have. Some of the common myths we come across from people who have never visited are pretty far fetched. The first myth is that in Canada all people or at least most of us live in igloos. Secondly, some people believe there is snow everywhere all year long; and thirdly, the Canadian policemen are all Mounties who dress everyday in their red uniforms. If the person who was making these remarks really took the time to study and understand our country they would know that this is not true. These are just assumptions based on someone else's observations of Canada and not factually proven.

I want to talk about some myths that have been damaging our families, our ministries and our communities. I want to address the myths about women specifically as these myths can often cause friction or a breakdown of the family unit. This book is all about balancing our family and ministry and these things need to be addressed so we can restore the rightful place of the woman as she is called to be. So others may see her as God sees her, without stigma or myths attached to her.

Myths about Women in the Family

It is important to talk about the myths attached to the woman in her family. I want to touch on two very damaging myths that have hindered women in their relationships and in their walk with the Lord.

Myth # 1: A Woman should only wash and cook and clean the home.

This is a myth that has been created from misinterpreting or misreading what God has to say in Genesis 2:18-25. In this scripture

God tells Adam that He will make him a "helpmate". The term helpmate has been misunderstood to mean that the woman is a domestic slave, bound to the home and to this role assigned to her. God did not mean for us to interpret this scripture this way. The Greek word used her for helpmate is often translated as "companion". What image comes to mind when you think of a companion? A companion is one who walks beside you and who shares in intimacy and partnership.

I love serving my husband and I do the household chores in the home with the help of my children. But often he will offer to help or surprise me with acts of service around the house. He has not bound me to the home, neither has he ever given the impression that this is all that I can do for him and the children. In fact he has frequently pushed me out of that role and encouraged me to step out in roles that normally would make me uncomfortable. He believes in me not only as a mother and wife but as a woman of God and loves to see me grow this way. Because of this we share a partnership in all areas. We partner in intimacy, we partner in companionship and we partner in ministry.

I enjoy teaching men and women about the stereotypes we place on ourselves and others. Too many people are bound by them and cannot move forward as God desires. As we begin to understand who we are as men and woman of God, then nothing can stop us or hold us back. We can begin breaking these stereotypes and limits placed on us by others or even ourselves. When we have our minds open and willing to receive what God has for us we will begin to see ourselves as God sees us.

Culture may dictate how we see ourselves or our mate. Although culture may be good when seen as a heritage for your children or a way of identifying your family unit it can also cripple the growth you have as a family. Sometimes we expect certain things from each other as a couple which may have been from a culture of the past and may not work for the good of the relationship of today. A prime example is the myth we are addressing right now. In many cultures, the woman is expected to be at home cooking and cleaning and taking care of the children. That is all that is expected of her, no more or no less. Yet financially the husband may be struggling to make ends meet and may even be out of work. What is wrong with this picture? I believe there are seasons in our lives as individuals and as companions on all levels.

When my husband and I were struggling with our young family, and he was still in school, I was out of the home, helping where I could to bring income into the home. That was one season. Another season was when my husband was doing a lot of missions and travelling. For that particular year he was gone two weeks out of each month. I had to run the business we started, work outside and was homeschooling the two youngest children. It was a season in our life where we had to adjust our mindsets and work together as a couple to meet the needs of our home. I have been blessed to be able to be home with the children for most of their formative years. But I am open to serving my husband and family in any capacity to see their needs met and to see them successful in all areas of life.

If we allow culture to dictate our relationship we will struggle and fight for a balance. Our way of looking at things may be outdated and out of place for the relationship we are in. We need to look to the Holy Spirit for direction and accountability. My husband and I come from two different cultural backgrounds.

We have learned to find the uniqueness in both and use only that which will complement the other. The first year we were married I think my husband was stunned to realize I only knew how to cook three or four dishes. The worst part of it was that it was all food that he did not like. Well I learned to adjust and received the best instruction on cooking from my husband. I am blessed to have a mother-in-law who taught her son how to cook from a young age. Not just cook but cook very well. So over the first years I gradually learned some new "Trinidad" dishes and expanded my knowledge. I could have just stuck to my culture of Dutch food dishes but as I learned to adapt to new food I soon found out it was very tasty. We enjoy the wonderful Dutch baking and some favourite dishes like "Sunday soup" as part of our family unit but equally enjoy the spicy curry meat and roti dishes from Trinidad. We did not allow culture to dictate how we ran our home and family. We blended our culture and made something very unique and quite wonderful. New ideas and new methods are birthed from an openness to learn and expand.

Myth # 2: Woman should be the doormat in a relationship.

Statistics show that in every part of the world, in the area of relationships many women have been misunderstood, abused, and their lives destroyed. There is a terrible epidemic of abuse and death, seeking to put down the spirit of a woman. It is nothing new. From the very beginning of time she has been blamed, lied to and discouraged from taking her place as a woman of substance and virtue.

Starting in the Garden of Eden, the woman was given the promise that one day their seed would bruise the head of the serpent. The devil has been hard at work trying to destroy that seed of hope. It is something that God has put in place for the woman for her to be a part of the redemption for mankind. It is meant to be a seed of hope for her and for the generations after her.

As couples come into our clinic for counselling I see the same look of hopelessness on the women's faces. There is also a look of desperation and a hunger for just a glimpse or glimmer of hope. They are looking for answers to a myth that has been clinging to them for centuries. How do we restore their hope, their desire for more than just surviving a relationship?

Statistics tell us that violence against women is a universal phenomenon. Women are subjected to different forms of violence such as physical, sexual, psychological and economic abuse. According to World Bank data, "Women aged 15-44 are more at risk from rape and domestic violence than from cancer, motor accidents, war and malaria".[6]

When we study the patterns of abuse of women worldwide we see customs that have been culturally accepted for generations put pressure on women to accept their abuse. These women accept being beaten by their husbands for very trivial reasons such as burning the food or arguing, or even leaving the home for short periods of time without telling their husband; they believe these infractions are grounds for receiving a punishment. The sad thing is that many of these women feel they deserve such treatment and think that the physical abuse is their fault.

Globally surveys have been taken that suggest half of all women who die from homicide are killed by their current or former husbands or partners. This means that close and intimate relationships that women have are the most dangerous to her health. I would like to see those statistics turned around. What can we do to strengthen our relationship so that a woman is encouraged, loved and appreciated for who she is as a woman of God? That instead of being a statistic of hopelessness and despair she can be part of a statistic that sees her in healthy, long-lasting relationships. Changing people's perceptions or ideas of who a woman is in a relationship will make the biggest difference.

The psalmist tells us, *"I will praise You, for I am fearfully and wonderfully made; marvellous are Your works, and my soul knows very well." Psalm 139:14.* We are fearfully and wonderfully made in the image of God, both male and female. He sees worth in us, worthy enough to be made in His image. Although as male and female we may play different roles in our relationships, we are still equal in the eyes of God. That is why God tells us that the two will become one when we commit ourselves before the Lord. We will become one in heart, mind and soul. We will respect one another and honor each other even as God honors us in our relationship. There will be no room for any disrespect because in essence we will be disrespecting our own self and God. There will be no room for either person to be a "the doormat" in a relationship.

Once we learn and apply these simple steps of respect and honour we will see a big change in our relationships.

MYTHS OF COMMUNITY

The myths I will be addressing have a direct impact on the community that women are a part of. Surveys tell us that there are approximately 57 million more women than men in the world.

Of course there are some exceptions like China and India, countries with a surplus of men. Saying all this leads us to believe that woman have and will make a great impact on our communities.

Myth #1: Women must stay home with the children and not work outside the home.

Although there has been much increase in the percentage of women working in the labour industry, women continue to bear most of the responsibilities for the home. They care for the children and other dependent household members by preparing meals and doing chores in the home. Women spend at least twice as much if not more time as men on unpaid domestic work. This tells us that women who are working outside the home spend a huge amount of time on the double burden of paid work and family responsibilities. When you take into account all the unpaid work, women's total work hours are longer than men's in all areas. This accounts for the increase of stress and pressure upon the woman of the home.

With all this said why would we say it is a myth that women should stay home and not work? Would this not release her from the burden of working double time if not triple more than her husband? Although this may appear to have a hint of truth to it we must look at this myth from a different angle. As a woman, I know that every area that I work in and serve my family must be submitted first to the Holy Spirit for confirmation and guidance. This includes our career plans.

Many use Proverbs 31 as a defense of woman's place in the home, yet if you read the passage carefully you will see that the virtuous women of that day made clothes and sold them outside, bringing income into her home. She also went out to look at land and purchased it much like a real estate agent would do today. She was an industrious woman and used her giftings and talents to be a blessing to her family and home. It brought much favour to her household and a place of prominence to her husband.

It all comes back to teamwork again and the seasons God has us go through for growth and betterment of our relationship and family. We cannot place another burden on the woman for her choice of career or work ethic. We can only encourage women to make wise choices for their family and home. When we critically judge women who have to work outside the home we place another burden of guilt on them for their efforts in supporting the family. If we see that their choices are affecting their family in a negative way then we can gently encourage them to re-evaluate their situation and help them to re-adjust their schedules. This needs to be done in a caring and encouraging way that does not belittle them or show judgment.

Myth # 2: Women should not seek out careers

God has given us an abundance of gifts and talents that He wants to see being used for the glory of His name. The Bible is clear on what is to be done with these gifts. As Jesus shared in the parable of the talents in Matthew 25, the wise use of gifts and the abilities entrusted to us by God, results in greater opportunities and brings glory to the gift giver. If we neglect the gifts we will lose more opportunities and even lose that which was given or entrusted to us. Men and women have been given gifts equally and both are responsible to use them and multiply them to the best of their ability.

Women have a prevalent role in the healthcare field today. Many of our caregivers and service providers in the community are women and we see a strong gifting of leadership and caring flowing through the system as they lead. Without their leadership and support we would see a failing healthcare system in our community. When women commit their careers to the Holy Spirit and allow His leading to balance their career and home they are only being obedient by using the gifts God has given them.

We have to be careful not to judge others for their choice of career pathway. We do not want to be a part of hindering the call of God or placing a negative stigma on a woman without knowing her relationship with God. We instead need to celebrate and accept ourselves as women of God, women who will make a mark on our communities and our society. God does not put limitations on us regarding our gifts; the sky is the limit. We limit ourselves by our attitudes and preconceptions of how we as women fit the various roles we play.

Let's celebrate and embrace our uniqueness and stir up our gifts so we can minister one to another. *"Therefore I remind you to stir up the gift of God which is in you through the laying on of my hands."* I Timothy 1:6 and another good scripture, *"As each one has received a gift, minister it to one another, as good stewards of the manifold grace of God."* 1 Peter 4:10

MYTHS OF CHURCH AND MINISTRY

Myth # 1: Women should be quiet in church

Where does this teaching originate? Why has this been such a big issue in the church? When we go to the scripture that has been interpreted to give us this impression, we have to understand the culture and people Paul was addressing when he wrote these words. *"Let a woman learn in silence with all submission. And I do not permit a woman to teach or to have authority over a man, but to be in silence. For Adam was formed first, then Eve. And Adam was not deceived, but the woman being deceived, fell into transgression. Never less she will be saved in childbearing if they continue in faith, love and holiness, with self-control."* 1 Timothy 2:11-15

Paul was specifically dealing with the Gnostics. There was a huge conflict between the early Christians and the Gnostics that can be similar to the church today and the New Age movement. Christians saw the Gnostics as enemies of the truth. Gnostics normally accepted the idea of salvation and of a supreme God and of a heavenly realm in action but instead of seeing body and spirit as a united thing, they separated out the material understanding of the world from the spiritual understanding.

They would not claim Jesus was fully human; anything merely human was distasteful to them. The miraculous, the spiritual and the mysterious were acceptable to them. They tended to see people in three spiritual planes. The upper class lived by a special knowledge. The lower class lived by faith. The spiritually disadvantaged were just not capable of "getting it". It is obvious in what class the Gnostics would place anyone who didn't agree with their assessment.

Gnostics claimed to have secret, hidden knowledge. They taught detailed genealogies and myths about their beginnings, giving exaggerated positions to Adam and Eve as well as others. Eve allegedly received hidden knowledge when she ate from the tree of knowledge. The Gnostics capitalized on this and instead of calling the act sin, they exalted it, and her. It became a major part of their teachings. Women were given a place of prominence and it was greatly misused as a result of the Gnostic teaching. Creating more vile flesh by having children was considered evil. Women who give birth will be hindered from entering Gnostic heaven

Gnostic women were promising godliness in exchange for good works. They based their deluded teachings on the myths and speculations of a "superior knowledge" through Eve. This is why Paul refers to Adam and Eve to refute this in chapter 2:13, 14. Eve fell first, she was deceived first; Paul was showing the Gnostics that Adam was made first. He was coming against the Gnostic teaching.

The book of Timothy tells us, *"Let a woman learn…"* *1 Timothy 2:11* The Judaizers said it was sin for a woman to learn the law but Paul was saying, "Don't stop them but let them learn. Why would Paul want them to learn? He wanted them to learn so that they would know the truth!

Gnostic women were teaching but they were operating in error and confusion. The type of learning that was taking place at that time was a type of question and answer format with heated debates and discussions. People would state their point of view while teaching was taking place creating a lot of confusion and noise. Therefore he finished "let them learn" with "in silence".

We need to ask ourselves, was Paul suggesting total silence? Silence (hesuchios) is the same word used in 1 Tim. 2:2 where it is translated as peaceableness. This means to refrain from meddlesome speech and to live free from arguments, strife, stress and turmoil. [4]

Paul allowed Priscilla to teach (Acts 18:26) so why would he be contradicting himself?

He is talking in the context of "those women professing godliness", the Gnostic women.

Ephesus was the home of the shrine of the goddess Diana. It was a very unclean city with women being involved in temple prostitution. When these women converted over to Christianity they had to learn new ways of dressing and adorning themselves. They could no longer dress to lure or tempt men.

Gnostics used sexual practices to bind the divine and the flesh together. Peter was also aware of this in 2 Peter 2:1, 14-18. *"For when they speak great swelling words of emptiness, they allure through the lusts of the flesh, through licentiousness..."*

Paul tells us that the woman will some day be restored and be able to teach. This is possible because childbearing, by producing the seed who destroyed Satan's power, balances the superior position of man established in the creation order. However, women can only be restored as they walk in faith and holiness.

Women were not told that they must stop teaching because they were females or women, but because they were in error; they were heretics.

When I think of women of the Bible such as Hannah, I am reminded of how she was perceived to be drunk and was rebuked by the high priest Eli. She had just made a vow to God, pouring out her heart and soul, committing her life and that of her son if He would just look upon her and remember her. Her request was for God to give her a son of her own, one she would dedicate to the Lord all the days of his life. Her prayer and her countenance were misunderstood by the high priest and yet she did not allow this to stop her from addressing the high priest. She spoke. She stood up for herself for she knew her innocence and knew her God. As soon as Eli saw her for who she was, he immediately told her to go in peace for the God of Israel will grant her petition.

Women are to be released from the misconceptions and misunderstandings put upon them. When we realize our position and our authority in Christ we can be effective in our church as a voice, a voice that is not silenced. We can be a voice that is respectful to those in authority and submissive to the Holy Spirit.

Myth # 2: Women should not teach, preach or minister to men or be on the pulpit.

As we have already addressed in the previous myth, the word of God does in no way refuse women to teach or preach. But it does warn and caution us in how we go about bringing the word and in what spirit.

It is actually kind of humorous that I would be writing on this topic as I hid from pastors, churches and my husband in regards to teaching or preaching. I have never sought to be in the pulpit or in the spotlight of ministry; I have for most of my life avoided it like the plague. Very slowly I began to understand some of the gifts that God has given me and though I did not want to I began stepping out. I realized that I had a responsibility to be all that I could be for God. He wanted all of me, and I had to release some of my fear and allow Him to move through me. I still find it difficult to believe that people want me to minister in their conferences or missions. But I am gradually seeing the purposes and plans God has for my life concerning ministry and the family.

Acts 2 tells us that in the last days God will pour out His Spirit upon ALL flesh! This includes man, woman and child. When God pours out His Spirit miracles happen. We will dream dreams, see visions, and prophesy; young men, old men, sons, daughters, menservants and maidservants will be involved. God sees us all and is no respecter of persons. He will use anyone who is willing and available, a vessel emptied of pride and doubt but ready to be filled by His Spirit and empowered with His Word. The emptier the vessel, the more it can be filled, and as we step out with the Spirit and Power we give it out to empower others, and then the cycle of refilling begins afresh.

Women should have the same privileges and opportunities as men because of what Jesus accomplished on the cross. His sacrifice also freed women so they would no longer be considered second class citizens. *"In Christ now there is neither bond nor free, Scythian nor Barbarian, male nor female; all are one in Christ Jesus."* Galatians 3:28

When Jesus visited Martha and Mary He was affirming women's new position. Martha was complaining to Jesus about Mary neglecting to help her serve. She even asks if Jesus cares that Mary has left her to serve alone requesting that Jesus tell Mary to help her. Jesus challenged her by telling her that Mary has chosen the better thing to do. *And Jesus answered and said to her, "Martha, Martha, you are worried and troubled about many things.*

163

But one thing is needed, and Mary has chosen that good part, which will not be taken away from her." Luke 10:41-42

This was challenging the culture of that day for only the men were allowed to sit learning from other men. Jesus was considered a bit of a radical but He was just introducing the new role of the woman that would be revealed after His death and resurrection.

Jesus also talked to the woman at the well which was not allowed, for the women could not speak to a man unless their husband was present. Jesus saw someone in need and ministered to her even as he would a man. *"And at this point His disciples came, and they marveled that He talked with a woman; yet no one said, "What do You seek?" or, "Why are You talking with her?"* John 4:27

This was another radical act that Jesus did during a time of confusion and limitations concerning women. His disciples marvelled that He talked with this woman but no one questioned Him or confronted Him. They had been following Him for years and must have seen a pattern forming concerning His ministry to women. He brought change to a very male domineering society and did it in such a gracious and compassionate way.

The Bible tells us that God gives gifts to people, and makes it clear that we ought not to neglect the gift that is in us. We are accountable to use what He has given us to the best of our ability so that it will bring glory to His name. If a woman has the gift of preaching, to neglect that gift is sinful. It does not come any simpler than that. I believe that there have been many women with the gift of preaching/teaching who have been pushed into a corner and told they are rebellious or feminists if they step out in their calling from God. We have lost many a good preacher or teacher because of this and this becomes a hindrance to the great commission and harvest of souls for God's kingdom.

As a woman steps out in her calling to preach or teach I believe that she needs to be continually mentored by other women and men. We do not need to prove anything to society or work harder just to make an impression. We just need to be humble and obedient to the call of God and allow others to speak into our lives as the Holy Spirit leads. The most important quality is to be teachable; for if we decide to become lone riders we open ourselves to the danger of being misled and misguided by our perceptions or thoughts. When we see the Word of God taking affect and rooting in people's hearts we can be assured that God is moving through us. We should be careful to continue to give Him the glory and not take the glory for ourselves.

Myth # 3: Women are to support their husband's ministry, not to minister with him

In the last number of years, I have seen a surprisingly small amount of husband and wife pastors preaching together in the pulpit. Although the concept is still fairly new, the power that is behind this is quite dynamic. Not only do you have two using their talents and giftings to bring forth a message relating to both men and women but a husband and wife ministering together. It brings a wonderful picture to the people you are ministering to of a working relationship in a marriage. The unity and strength that is utilized and portrayed through this couple will encourage others to step out in their gifts.

My husband and I have wonderful pastors who preach together regularly. It was quite new for some people coming into the church and may have taken some adjustment in their thinking and perceptions. We see a unit, a force, a team, a ministry and a marriage all wrapped up in this dynamic duo. It is a model in our lives that we needed to help us in our ministry together.

What we see happening in many ministries today is the rampant spread of adultery amongst the staff working every day together doing God's work. The pastor falls into adultery with the worship pastor or Sunday school director. The youth pastor with the secretary or the co-pastor and the list goes on. They are working together every day with the pressures of ministry and the emotional turmoil that it may produce. Who do you talk to or, who do you spend the most time with? These are the people who you may let down your guard around and allow yourself to make the biggest mistake of your life. One you may never have dreamed or imagined anything could happen. It just happened; the time was right, the opportunity was there and before you knew it you let down your guard. Once that happens it becomes easier and easier to slip until you have fallen so far down that you cannot see a way out.

When a husband and wife minister together there is a protection clause that covers them. They are accountable to each other not only in their marriage but in their ministry. It truly narrows the margin by which the devil can intervene with adultery and fornication. They become an unstoppable force that is forged together in spirit, faith and body.

The scripture tells us, *"So God created man in His own image; in the image of God He created him; male and female He created them. Then God blessed them, and God said to them, "Be fruitful and multiply; fill the earth and subdue it; have dominion over the fish of the sea, over the*

birds of the air, and over every living thing that moves on the earth".
Genesis 1; 27&28

God has from the very beginning of the world intended man and woman to rule together. He created us in His very own image, male and female. Not only did He create us in His image but He blessed us. When I think of that particular moment when God laid His blessing upon the man and woman I imagine the joy and power of that moment. The Creator, blessing that which He created, was giving them dominion over the fish, the birds and every living thing. He also said to be fruitful and multiply - the command to have children and fill the earth. Everything God said concerning that which He created was for the benefit of both man and woman. There is a true partnership pattern shown here and I believe it extends even now to ministering as a couple as well.

POINTS TO PONDER

- *Have you considered the myths placed on women today that have been passed down from generations but have no bearings or standing for today? What do you feel God's word says about that?*

- *What limitations or myths have you had to deal with? How did you cope or what did you do to conquer or dispel the myth?*

- *God's word gives us the pattern for partnership between man and woman in Genesis 1:27,28. Can you see this partnership benefiting the church? Give some examples.*

12 THE LEGACY

When I picture myself as one individual among billions of people here on this earth I think about my responsibility as a child of God. What am I doing that stands out in the crowd; what am I doing that will make an impact in my family, community and church? What makes me different than anyone else here on earth that when I leave this earth I will be remembered for leaving a legacy behind?

The fact that we are children of the most high means we are blood-bought, Holy Ghost-filled and given every gift and resource possible from our heavenly Father. This should inspire us to reach for the stars. There are no limits in how far we can go or reach when we are so fully equipped. The only one who can limit us is ourselves.

The Bible tells us that, *"The memory of the righteous is blessed, but the name of the wicked will rot"*. Proverbs 10:7

We have to truly understand that as a righteous person we can even in memory be blessed. We live in a world today in which humanity is more concerned about our own needs than the needs of others. Selfishness and personal ambition is put on the front burner and anyone or anything that gets in the pathway to success is cast aside or rejected, sacrificed at the altar of personal ambition. The word of God tells us clearly in Proverbs that the name of the wicked will rot, meaning die and be forever forgotten. When something rots it gives off a distinct and foul smell and creates a picture in your mind of death and decay. It does not last, but decays and nothing of lasting value is left behind.

On the other side of the picture is the memory of the righteous; it is blessed. Blessing is something that builds up, inspires and multiplies itself, extending to others and their loved ones. It is a fragrance of health, life and of hope. What fragrance do you want to leave for your loved ones?

1. FAMILY

"A good man leaves an inheritance to his children's children, but the wealth of the sinner is stored up for the righteous". Proverbs 13:22

Leaving an inheritance, a legacy behind for your children can encompass so many things. A legacy left behind can be material possessions, mementos, and memories that are forever etched in the minds and hearts of those left behind. There are many personal belongings that have a special event or thought attached to them that when inherited bring great joy and comfort.

But I want to focus more on the legacy that you can leave behind that is much simpler and more generational. As parents we dream about all the things that we want our children to remember us by; we can plan their future, careers and future family planning. This is good but we need to remember that every day we are building a legacy, a legacy that may or may not have been intentional. The little things that we say or do with our children on a day to day basis may be the very thing that they remember for future generations. Have I created a safe place for them, a place of peace and serenity? Have they felt that they can share any of their feelings with me whether big or small? Am I listening to their hopes and dreams or have I allowed the busyness of the world to take precedence?

I remember the years when I was a small child, growing up in a Godly home. One of the things that I remember clearly about my parents that has impacted me the most was their prayer time. I recall one particular time when for a reason I cannot remember now I happened to open their bedroom door in the evening while they were preparing for bed. I found them both kneeling by their bed praying so I quickly and quietly shut the door. I am not sure if they saw me or not but that one moment, that one picture is so engraved in my mind that it still has a strong effect on me. I know that they prayed daily for us but that image confirmed it for me.

What image has been engraved in the mind of my children? Have I been an example of all that I have taught or instructed in the home? These are the questions I ask to help remind myself to be the model of what I teach, not to be just the instructor. Anybody can be the instructor, as the world is ready to equip and teach our children in any way they see fit. I want to be their model; I want to be the one to inspire them, to encourage them, to be the one they look up to for advice and instruction.

As we talk about the family I would like to incorporate three methods of leaving a legacy behind for our children, and their children, and their children's children.

1. *Faith*

2. *Mentorship*

3. *Friendship*

FAITH

The most valuable deposit you can impart to your children and family is your identity in Jesus Christ. When you deposit spiritually into your family you deposit a seed of truth that not only will grow and strengthen their lives but will be a legacy to pass down to their children.

When your children have a large deposit of faith living and growing inside of them this in turn helps to lead and guide them in their decisions of present and future. It is a legacy that will define who they become as a person and who they will influence because of their faith.

Faith is said to be like a mustard seed, that though it is the smallest of seeds it grows and matures to be a tree of great use and beauty. It grows up to the maximum of 20 feet and because of its low height is often used for landscaping and beautifying homes in hot dry climates. The branches grow very low to the ground so it provides much needed shade in the hot countries it is found in. The birds of the air find refuge in its low branches. The mustard tree has may other uses. Its branches have been used in some communities as toothbrushes. The branches contain an ingredient that can resist bacteria and plaque. The mustard tree also produces a fruit that is edible and is very nutrient filled; even the seeds can be eaten. The tree shoots are edible as well so you can see that this tree fills many needs of humanity.

Now going back to faith, if faith is like a mustard seed and that seed grows into something that provides so much for humanity, what are we doing to see that seed of faith take root in our children's lives? If that deposit of faith we impart as a mother or father can make such an impact as it grows, we can see it also being passed down as a legacy of faith for our children's children.

How do we deposit faith you may ask? *"The fear of the Lord is the beginning of wisdom, and the knowledge of the Holy One is understanding."* Proverbs 9:10

There are many ways we can instill faith in our children. We know that as we teach our children to pray we encourage a relationship between God and themselves. They will learn to have faith in God who hears their prayers and learn to trust Him as He answers. Teaching the Word of God in a real and tangible way will create in them a hunger to know more. Family devotions where all members are encouraged to participate will gently push them to study and speak their thoughts concerning the Word of God for their lives. Knowing that their thoughts and opinions matter will allow them to blossom in their faith.

During our family devotions one evening we found out something very important about one of our daughters. We were reading from a daily devotional book written by Charles Spurgeon that we had recently started using for our family devotion time. The chapter we read that day was called "the power of your story" and it talked about how the story of our Christian faith is unique, individual and distinctive. That it is a story of "personal experience" - what God did personally in your life. We read the questions at the end of the devotion and everyone participated. When we came to a particular question we asked everyone at the table to answer it. The question was: Why can a person's personal story, even a simple one, be a powerful influence for God? [8] Some talked about their stand for Christ in school, another about their prayer for friends. Gradually as we went around the table we heard personal stories of faith and the influence it had on them and others.

It had now reached one of our daughters who began to share with us how she was bullied in school. She shared some experiences she had, some that she had never shared with anyone before. She tearfully explained how this experience marked her and how she decided to stand up and not allow herself to be bullied again. As she shared about her experience it answered a lot of questions for us about her recent behaviour in the home. She was meticulous about her weight and exercise and she became more vocal in her response to disagreements with siblings. It helped us understand the reason for her behaviour and to be empathetic to her.

Sharing personal stories of your success and failures in your walk of faith will also help instill faith in your children. There are times that we as a family will be sitting around, just relaxing and we will begin talking about old times where God brought us through some tough situations. We will reminisce about the past and without realizing it we will be depositing faith into our children's hearts. We can use our experiences to teach on how to make the right decisions in life.

The Bible tells us, *"Your word I have hidden in my heart, that I might not sin against You."* Psalm 119:11

The word of God has the power to enable you to resist sin. Teaching our children how to hide God's word in their hearts will empower them to resist the enemy. We protect our children and equip them when we teach them how to hide God's word in their heart. When we speak the word over their lives at a very young age it will become a part of them. We can also encourage scripture memory through songs, games or books to help them deposit the word of God into their hearts. I have spoken God's word over our children even while they were still in my womb. I prayed for their health, their ministry and even for their future spouse. We need to remember that God's Word is a powerful and life-giving force. The Bible tells us that it is living and powerful and even sharper than any two-edged sword (Hebrews 4:12). Our children are our frontline ministry obligation and mission. Without them we will have a testimony that will be weak and feeble and our fruit will be of a lesser quality.

We can be effective in ministry to some extent without the testimony of our children's lives. But when you compare an apple tree that is laden down with heavy and ripe fruit to a tree that just holds its own and brings forth a few apples you see the difference in ministry. When you are a family unit visible in the community and the church you are seen as such; you are not seen as individuals. Can you see the need for ministry at home first and then the world? The world is looking at you as a family unit and we are responsible to God to be a good witness and steward of what He has given us.

We cannot change the past mistakes we have made concerning our children but we can change the future through our grandchildren and the adoption of spiritual sons and daughters. *"As His divine power has given us all things that pertain to life and godliness, through the knowledge of Him who called us by glory and virtue."* 2 Peter 1:3

We can take God's word and impart knowledge of it so He will in turn give us all things that pertain to life and godliness. Peter gives us that hope in the scripture that as we obtain knowledge of Him, His divine power will give us <u>all things,</u> all the things that pertain to life in Him.

We have a command from God, telling us that we must continue in the things we have learned. *"But you must continue in the things which you have learned and been assured of, knowing from whom you have learned them, and that from childhood you have known the Holy Scriptures, which are able to make you wise for salvation through faith which is in Christ Jesus."* 2 Timothy 3:14,15

We can only continue if we have already learned them; that is it has been a part of us as we have grown in our spiritual walk. We are wise to prepare our children at a young age to learn scripture for we are promised that it will make them wise for salvation through faith in Jesus.

I pray that this is your hope and desire, to see your children grow and mature in their faith, that they may be a witness of God's faithfulness and goodness. That they may continue in all that you have taught them about faith in God and following His footsteps. This is a legacy to leave behind for your children. A legacy that no man can steal, but it can only grow and extend to future generations.

MENTORSHIP

You can make time to sit down and talk with your children about the things of God which are important but in order to be effective you need to be a role model. They need to see you in action, modeling the very truths you are teaching them. This way they will not only know the truths of Gods Word but understand them. Truths can only be understood when they are lived out.

Mentorship begins from the day your child enters this world until your golden years. From birth to marriage to grandchildren we will continue to be an example to our children.

Mentorship inspires Leadership…which inspires Greatness….which inspires the World!

In what areas can we be a mentor to our children?

1. *Relationships – from friendship to courtship we can inspire our children to have healthy and lasting relationships.*

2. *Career – the example we set for education and training will inspire our children to choose careers that meet or succeed our own choices.*

3. *Health and Exercise – stimulating the mind includes healthy choices in diet and exercise. Our example as a parent living a healthy lifestyle sets goals and a pattern for them to follow for their future.*

4. *Self-Esteem – when we are confident and comfortable with who we are as a created being made in God's image we inspire confidence in our children.*

5. *Parenting – every decision, every moment, and every event is recorded in the recesses of our children's mind. We need to make every moment count and every experience be one that ends in a positive note.*

6. *Marriage – if we want our children to be in a happy and mutually satisfying relationship with their spouse we need to model such a marriage at home. Let that be your motivator if nothing else but to see a pattern of healthy marriages running through the generations of your family! If you come from line of unhealthy relationships, there is hope; you can break the pattern not only for yourself but for the future.*

7. *Faith – let your home be centered and secured on your faith. Incorporate family worship, devotions and personal prayer time. Mentor strong faith practices in the home to invest in your children's life of faith and worship.*

FRIENDSHIP

When we talk about friendship we must remember that being a friend to our children is one part of our relationship but there are many more parts for us to play that help balance our role as a parent. We must be a friend in the sense of listening; being the kind of person your child feels they can confide in and enjoy spending time with. But we must be also the parent in discipline and guidance in decision making. A parent should know the difference and be able to switch roles according to the needs.

Our children know that they can confide in us whenever they have an issue and as a friend we will listen and support them. But if they make decisions that negatively affect the family, themselves and those close to them then we may have to take charge and use our authority as a parent to help them to help themselves.

Friendship includes going out for coffee together, early morning walks or, taking them to the gym to work out even when you do not feel like it. It is being spontaneous and creative, taking unplanned road trips and excursions. Friendship is expressing in many various ways the joy of being together and your interest in their personal life.

In today's technical and media society there are many ways of communicating with your child. I often use my cell phone to text our children a word of encouragement, maybe a quick note saying, "I love you" or a short scripture. At times I will remind them of how much I appreciate them, or thank them for the little things they have done to bless my life. This is part of a friendship relationship; giving compliments, words of praise and encouragement, show that you care about their lives and what goes on each day. You have to remind yourself daily of the importance of developing and maintaining a relationship with your children.

There are times that I have become overwhelmed with the emotional and physical demands of each of our children. They are such unique individuals and at times have persistently brought some personal request or interest that demands my attention. I may feel inadequate in meeting each of our seven children's personal interests and sometimes my brain cannot process all the data that comes at me at one time. Does this ever happen to you? I know women are said to have a brain that functions like a ball of wire and we remember every event and what each event is connected to. It is like electric current moving from one wire to the next and reconnecting it all back to the start. That may be true in most cases but I think sometimes there can be an overload of information that builds up overtime and causes a short circuit. Maybe it's just me, but it happens and my mind goes blank for a short time. My children will look at me to answer their "very important to them" question or request and will be stunned to see me sputter to get my words out and then nothing… Mind you it lasts only for a moment but it happens. When this occurs I find something to do that clears my mind and helps me focus to be effective as a mother and friend. I am sure you know what works best for you to clear your mind. If you don't then find something to help you relax.

We need to be real with our children as we cannot expect our lives to be perfect. We will experience rocky and rough roads ahead but as we learn to work together and maintain a friendship, we know that we will soon hit a smooth patch.

Friendship involves some sacrifice of self as we seek to reach our children at their emotional and spiritual level. We may be older, have lots of experience in relationships and life in general but we need to put ourselves in their shoes and help them where they are at. Too many times we want to solve their problems with our great advice and wisdom when all they really want is a listening ear. Friendship is listening, putting our own feelings aside and getting down in the trenches with our children.

Friendship with your children will motivate them to keep coming home even after they have become an adult. They will not be counting the days to leave home but will be returning as a student, with their spouse, and with their children. It will be a family with open doors and open hearts.

POINTS TO PONDER:

- *When is the last time you went out with your child and enjoyed a night of fun and laughter? Have you ever taken the time to think about what it would be like to be in your child's shoes, experiencing their daily life experiences?*

- *Can you name at least three things each of your children enjoys doing the best?*

- *Plan a special day of doing something your child enjoys and use this opportunity to be a part of their joy and laugh along with him or her.*

- *Let it be your goal to work to be the parent of whom your children might say, "Her children rise up and call her blessed" (Proverbs 31:28) and "His children are blessed after him". (Proverbs 20:7)*

2. COMMUNITY

Today we see and hear our young people crying out for a hero. They want a hero to adore, to follow, to mimic, to understand them and what they are going through and to change their lives. They chase after the dream of being just like their hero, from the clothes they wear to the food they eat, wanting to taste success and prestige but more importantly wanting to be happy. But what heroes are they following? We can only see those that are visible through the media which comes at us from all sides. Have you seen the heroes/idols that are visible today? Are you prepared for this generation to model themselves after lust, vanity, promiscuity, and self indulgence?

When I was a teenager I would follow certain bands and their music. I would belt out their songs with everything in me because I believed that they alone understood how I felt. Tears would be streaming down my cheeks as I related to the lyrics of the songs. But you know what, now that I remember, now that I think about it, those songs never solved my problems; those songs never changed my life and the direction I was heading. They just feed my emotions at that time. It was everyday, caring people with God's heart and a willingness to be used by Him who brought change to my life.

One summer, when I was 15 years old, I went to Redlands, California with my sister and her husband. They were training for 2 months at the MAF base, preparing for an overseas trip. I came along to babysit their two children for them while they were in classes for the day. My eyes were opened to another world of people, from all different churches but having a common faith. I met another young girl in the compound whose parents were also in training. She was only 12 years old and really the closest in age for me to relate to other than the smaller children. She became my friend and began to share with me her relationship with Jesus. I had grown up in church but did not realize that I needed to ask Jesus personally to be my Saviour. She began to urge me to make a commitment, so one day after putting the children for a nap I began to pray and weep and dedicate my life to Jesus. It was definitely a defining moment in my life. Yes, I made mistakes afterwards and it took a few years to get myself on track but that 12 year old girl is one of my heroes!! I had the pleasure of attending her wedding years later in Pennsylvania, still committed and serving Jesus.

Why am I talking about heroes? Well when talking about leaving a legacy in the community we have to look at who will impact lives. Who is going to make a difference in the community so that years later they will still be remembered as making an impact, a change for the better? Just as we believe we need to leave a legacy for our children, there is a need for us to do the same for our community. We want our legacy to benefit our community even after we are gone.

In the late 1700's there was a great reformer by the name of John Wesley who was born into a morally corrupt society. England was characterized by disease, gin and filthy living conditions. There was no running water or soap and life expectancy was an average of somewhere in the mid forties. The diseases that were found during this time like small pox and the plague had no cure. Working conditions were terrible with physical abuses rampant throughout the workplace. Children were allowed in the bars and given gin to keep quiet. Schools were not common and only the select and the rich were allowed to attend. Obviously in the midst of such conditions murder and suicide were common. History tells us that England was in such a bad state that it was not far away from revolution.

Here is a young man, eager and highly intelligent, living in these conditions who began preaching. He started to have great influence and became highly respected in his community. Through the many conversions in his ministry there were also social reforms. He began to preach a lot on cleanliness and holiness. People started taking better care of themselves because of his preaching. Physical abuse and swearing was greatly reduced because of his preaching on holiness. People even began to come to work on time. He founded Sunday schools that taught the children how to read and write and they also got to read the Bible.

In 1774 he wrote a book called, *"Thoughts Upon Slavery"* which proved to be one of the most far-reaching studies ever done on slavery. As his influence grew he became more influential in society. His book along with the fact that a lot of his Methodist followers made it into government contributed to the abolishment of slavery in 1807.

John Wesley is an example of a hero for society, for the community. He made such an impact that he left a legacy behind and it became a part of our history books. Not only did he preach the Word and bring lives to Christ but he changed the community around him. He imparted life to a dark and dreary time and brought light and restoration. He is a hero to the community. His contribution to society stopped a revolution from happening in England.

Being an advocate for your community can mean joining the local school council and doing your part to see that this generation of young people are receiving the best education and resources available. You can also be an advocate for the community food bank or shelter, using your skills and abilities to see the needs of the homeless and helpless being met. Maybe God is urging you to fight for the rights of the unborn and be an encouragement to those struggling with pregnancy and parenthood. What about all those struggling with their relationships within a marriage? Can you help couples talk about their issues and differences as male and female and give them hope? All these examples will eventually bring about a change or shift in the people you are helping. We do not always know the greater effect we are making and maybe will never know but God knows and He is the great rewarder to those who diligently seek Him.

One of the great benefits of being an advocate is that we do not become centered in ourselves as we begin to be benevolent. Our own world of "me and myself and I" has now expanded to the point that we tend to forget about our own little issues as they pale in comparison to what we now see or hear. When Jesus heard the news that John the Baptist had been beheaded he went out to a deserted place but the people followed Him. Although Jesus was experiencing great pain and sorrow he still was moved by compassion for the people and began to heal the sick till it became evening. Not only did He bring healing to the sick, but he also performed the miracle of feeding over five thousand people with five loaves and two fish. He put aside the, me, myself and I and used a time of great sorrow to produce miracles and healing.

When I think about Jesus and His ministry on earth, I think of how He was more than a teacher or preacher. He touched the people, he fed the people, and he healed and delivered them. He reached out to those around Him and met them where they were at, rich or poor, sinful or spiritual. He ministered to the community around Him and all those that met Him would remember what He did or said. It was a legacy that spread to each generation even to us all today. His was a legacy of love and forgiveness, hope and a future, restoration and unity. *"The wise shall inherit glory, but shame shall be the legacy of fools."* Proverbs 3:35

Joseph was a young man who through serving the Lord with all his heart saw an opportunity to help those that held him in bondage. He was a man who had a good reason to feel forsaken, forgotten or could have languished in the pits of despair. Joseph decided to put his trust in God and not allow his circumstances to rule his faith in God. He did something with the wisdom that God had given him and blessed the Egyptian community. Through the dreams that God had given him it was determined that a great famine was coming. Joseph began to help the Pharaoh organize the storage of food in preparation for the coming lean years. Because of Joseph's investment into the community that he lived in he saved an entire nation from starvation and these were the very people that imprisoned him. Joseph's sacrifice and investment also made a way for his family to benefit and be provided for during the famine.

God will always make a way for you when you look out for the needs of others. We never have to worry about our own circumstances. *"Therefore I say to you, do not worry about your life, what you will eat or what you will drink; nor about your body, what you will put on. Is not life more than food and the body more than clothing? Look at the birds of the air, for they neither sow nor reap nor gather into barns; yet your heavenly Father feeds them. Are you not of more value than they?"* Matthew 6:25, 26

POINTS TO PONDER:

- *What will people remember you for? What example are you setting for your community and the future of your community?*

- *What investment have you made that will reap such a harvest that even after you leave this earth it will continue to flourish and multiply?*

- *These are questions that we need to ask ourselves daily as we honour God, and seek His will for our lives.*

3. CHURCH

In 1844, Lisbon, Ohio a baby girl was born named Maria. At age 13 she became born again and as the preacher prayed for her he asked that her life might be a shining light. Maria heard the call of God upon her life but there was one thing that stood in her way. She was a woman and women were not even allowed to preach or even vote for that matter. She was determined though and decided that if she could not minister then she would have to marry a missionary to fulfill her call.

On the way to college she received the news that her father died on the farm. She had to return home and help support the family. She met and married a farmer and became Maria Woodworth Etter. She could not answer the call of the Lord with six children to raise and a husband who had no desire for ministry. Then she lost five of her six children to disease. Marie instead of becoming bitter towards God began searching for answers in the Word of God. She saw how God used women throughout the Bible and read how the spirit was poured out upon ALL flesh in the book of Joel. Then she had a vision where she was taken by angels into a great field of waving golden grain. She began to preach and saw the grains begin to fall like sheaves. In the midst of the vision Jesus spoke and told her that just as the grain fell, so people would fall as she preached. She could not longer deny the call of God and she answered yes to the call.

She began to minister first to her community and although she did not know what she was going to say God assured her that He would put the words in her mouth. As soon as she opened her mouth the crowd began to weep and fall on the ground, weeping and running out of the sanctuary with holy fear. This opened the door for her to different churches in her area for revival meetings and thus began her ministry.

She had a great love for different cultures and that also caused racial persecution for her ministry. She preached in many black churches and helped their preachers and also supported their revivals. She went into the Indian reservations and stayed there for weeks ministering to them and helping where she could. All were welcome in her home; whether they were black or white, rich or poor, she loved them all.

Marie became known as the revivalist that could break towns open. She was also called the Grandmother of the Pentecostal movement because of all the miracles and manifestations of God's power present in her ministry.

Why am I sharing all of this? I just wanted to give you an example of someone who left a legacy in her church. Future generations will remember the price she paid for women to minister in church. The manifestations that were present in her ministry started a pattern for future churches in reaching the lost and reviving those who had left the faith. There was no denying that God was at work here and all He needed was a yielded and willing vessel to be used by Him so His glory may be seen.

APOSTLE PAUL

Paul of Tarsus, who was formerly known by his Jewish name Saul, was a tent maker by trade, a Pharisee by faith and persecutor of the new Jewish sect called Christians. He was educated in the matters of Jewish law but heading in the direction of creating a legacy for himself of destruction, persecution and hatred. It was while on this pathway to destruction he found himself going to Damascus and he encountered the only person who could change his destiny, his legacy and that was Jesus.

This encounter was life changing, direction changing and provided for us Paul's written contribution to most of the New Testament. His encounter with Jesus led him to be one of the greatest missionaries of the Christian faith. Paul's journeys are recorded in the book of Acts, showing that he was one of the greatest leaders in the early missionary movement.

Paul was an unlikely candidate for this position. He was not sought out by the local leaders or apostles of the early church. In fact many of the leaders questioned his conversion and were fearful of him. They were hesitant to let him in their inner circle, into their confidence and into their faith. That's why the Lord gave a certain disciple named Ananias a vision, a vision to restore Saul's sight and baptize him in the faith. Ananias was fearful as well and questioned the Lord but then when the Lord replied in defense of Saul and called him a chosen vessel who would bear

His name, Ananias obeyed. Still the disciples were all afraid of him and could not believe that he was a disciple, a follower of Christ. It took a young man named Barnabas to introduce Saul to the group. Barnabas the encourager used his influence and faith to get acceptance for Saul.

God will use the most unlikely people to carry out His will and purpose. Who would have thought that a man like Saul, a persecutor of Christians would become Paul the apostle, a man who left one of the greatest legacies behind for the church? Almost half of the books of the New Testament are credited to his authorship and he is cited to be one of the greatest religious leaders of all time. He is responsible for spreading the Gospel through communities across the Roman Empire and established churches in Asia Minor and Europe.

This is quite a legacy to leave behind, one we may think we could never achieve or attempt to achieve. This is untrue as each and every one of us is called to service for our king. We may never know the impact of our contributions to the church. We cannot predict the outcome of the gifts we use to sow into the lives of those in the church. All we are called to do is be faithful to the call God has place upon our life and see that we have the right attitude in carrying it out.

Think about the impact you can have on future generations for being faithful in your service to the king of kings. Each service, each contribution, each heart touched is paving a legacy for your future and the future of your church. Don't sit idle as those around you are thriving in ministry. Allow God to use you as you are and step into some deep waters, having faith that He will direct your pathway.

POINTS TO PONDER:

- *What legacy are you leaving for future generations in the church?*

- *Can God be calling you in regards to ministry in the church, leaving lasting fruit and investments? Has He been speaking to you through your pastor or mentor?*

- *Has His Word confirmed to you the plan He has for you concerning the church and its ministries? What would He have you do today, now, at this moment?*

Do you hear Him? I know He is speaking to you at this moment. Why do I know this? It is because He has been the one to help me, lead me and inspire me to write this book for His glory and for the benefit of His children. Heed His call, for He desires to see you step into the ministry He has planned and ordained for you. It may feel like you are stepping out into the unknown but know that He is with you and with God by your side anything is possible. All things are possible!

13 FUTURE EXPECTATIONS

"Live for today, don't think about tomorrow." This is a motto by which many people live their lives, seeking only the thrill of that moment or the high of that day and not thinking about the repercussions of their actions or the outcome of their decisions. People often do not want to take responsibility for their future.

In our relationships we see husbands and wives succumbing to the one brief affair or one impulsive fling, seeking only to fill their emptiness or physical need with a quick fix or a cheap thrill, never allowing themselves to think about what comes next, who they are hurting or what problems they are creating for their future. It is only the thrill of the moment, but the moment comes and goes and with it comes an even deeper emptiness and a deep loneliness.

When I think of future expectations concerning our relationships, our family and our ministry I can only pray that we will have a strong desire to fight for our future. In order to fight we need to make some decisions on how to proceed and equip our-selves to fight for our relationships. As I pondered and studied the scripture I discovered that there are certain areas that we need to address and challenge ourselves on in order to see the future clearly.

1. CHOICES/HEDGES

In every area of life we are challenged with choices - choices in our careers, friendships, and our choice to give into temptation. From the very beginning God gave us a free will, and because of temptation Adam and Eve sinned. When given the opportu-nity to make the right choice and honour God their creator they failed, gave into their curiosity and sinned. Eve made a choice to take the place that was not hers, a place of authority and provision. She offered the apple to Adam when it was his God ordained place to provide for her. The serpent was very cunning in how he proceeded to orchestrate their downfall. Not only did they sin by disobeying God and His only requirement to not eat the fruit of the tree of good and evil but they also sinned in dis-obeying the order of the family unit in leadership of provision.

Earlier on in this book I shared how my husband told me that he chose to love me. It was a choice that he decided to never back down from. He chose to love me in spite of my many failures as a wife and mother. In spite of my weaknesses and shortcom-ings he chose to love me through it all. Now our love is stronger than ever because we have been through the fire, we have been refined through the burning process and something beautiful has emerged from it. This choice of his has paved the way for our future.

I believe that we have to intentionally make wise and healthy choices. Not all of us have come from strong and vibrant family units that encourage good choices. We may have to go against the norm or flow of what we have grown accustomed to. The important thing is that we have the choice to make the change. We can make or break the way for our future. It is all up to us.

I have sat in counselling sessions where either the husband or wife blames their behaviour on culture. This is just the way they grew up, this is just how their particular culture is, and therefore their behaviour is justified. Blame it on culture, don't blame it on me! This is not the way God wants us to lead our family. He continually gives us instructions on how to lead and how to be an example to our family, even if it means breaking the patterns of our past generations.

In the Bible Joshua had to address the Israelites concerning the ways of their fathers, their fathers who served other gods while they were in Egypt. He asked them to choose for themselves who they would serve. *"Now therefore, fear the Lord, serve Him in sincerity and in truth, and put away the gods which your fathers served on the other side of the River and in Egypt. Serve the Lord! And if it seems evil to you to serve the Lord, choose for yourselves this day whom you will serve, whether the gods which your fathers served that were on the other side of the River, or the gods of the Amorites, in whose land you dwell. But as for me and my house, we will serve the Lord."* Joshua 24:14,15

Can you see the bigger picture? We can either continue in the ways of our fathers because maybe it's just the only way we know or we are afraid to change, or we can chose a brighter pathway with a future for ourselves and our family. It is not impossible.

In fact all things are possible with Christ, for him who believes. We can overcome by the blood of the Lamb and the word of our testimony. Our God will make a way even when there seems to be no way. (Mark 9:23, Rev.12:11, Isaiah 43:16)

Joshua himself affirmed his position by declaring that as for himself and his family, they would serve the Lord. He spoke before all the tribes of Israel, their elders, judges and officers. It was a public declaration of the choice he made in spite of his forefather's mistakes and failures in serving the true and living God. Our declarations and our public confession of our decisions will hold us accountable to those we speak them to. Just like my husband's decision to choose to love me. I will hold him accountable to those words because he spoke them to me from the very start of our marriage.

Speak forth that which you want for your future; chose to make choices that will pave the way for a better future for you, your family and your family's family.

2. HOPE

"For I know the thoughts that I think towards you, says the Lord, thoughts of peace and not of evil, to give you a future and a hope." Jeremiah 29:11

When I think of hope a few things come to mind. I can mentally visualize a picture of my little index finger peeking out above the water. There is still hope if my finger can be seen above the water of life that has me totally immersed. It is an image I carry with me to remind me that in every situation, through every trial and turn in life, there is always hope.

God reminds us in Jeremiah that we have a future and a hope in Him. This tells me that in order for me to be future oriented I must have hope. It must be alive in me and motivate me to forge ahead. God's thoughts towards me are not of evil but are thoughts of peace. If God is thinking of me with thoughts of peace, to give me a future and a hope then what can stop me?

This reminds me of the prophet Elijah who was told by God that rain was coming during a time of severe famine in Samaria. *"And it came to pass after many days that the word of the Lord came to Elijah, in the third year, saying, "Go, present yourself to Ahab, and I will send rain on the earth. So Elijah went to present himself to Ahab; and there was a severe famine in Samaria."* 1 Kings 18:1-2

Elijah told King Ahab that there was a sound of abundance of rain. Although not a drop of rain was seen he climbed to the top of Mount Carmel and prostrated himself to the ground with his face between his knees. Let's read what happens next. *"And said to his servant, "Go up now look toward the sea." So he went up and looked, and said, "There is nothing." And seven times he said, "Go again." Then it came to pass the seventh time that he said, "There is a cloud, as small as a man's hand, rising out of the sea!" So he said, "Go up, say to Ahab, prepare your chariot, and go down before the rain stops you."* 1 Kings 18:43-44

Elijah had hope brimming inside of him. He climbed the mountain and set himself in a position of prayer. Then he began to send his servant out. The servant went once, twice, three times, each time returning with no news. But hope was not deterred by the servant's report. Hope does not give up when there is no answer as yet on the horizon. Hope does not quit when the report is unfavorable. The servant was sent seven times and finally on that seventh time he saw a cloud as small as a man's hand rising out of the sea. Hope now had a sign; it was not big and it was not a sure thing but Elijah knew that hope would bring about the desired result.

There are many instances when we try to put hope into action. We confess God's Word, we pray, we hope but we don't allow God to do His work in His own time frame. We may hope for a short time and then give up when we do not see the results right away. Or, we may hope for an extended period of time and see some signs of hope along the path way, but don't recognize them or hold on to them like we should. We may not see the small cloud rising out of the sea because we are too focused on seeing the answer come in a bigger package and don't recognise the signs.

A good example is the relationship between a husband and wife. She hopes that he will show her more attention or appreciate her as a woman. She has an ideal picture in her mind of what he needs to do and how he needs to do it. He comes home early one night to spend some much needed time with his wife. He knows he has been busy and wants to make it up to her. But as soon as he opens the door she bombards him with some issue or dispute in the home. She decides to bring up the topic of his neglecting her and words fly out of her mouth without thought or care. She hasn't taken note of his early arrival, she hasn't given him time to explain and she attacks his character unnecessarily.

If she had been giving hope a chance she would have seen this as a sign, a sign of hope in his making an effort to be home early with her.

I believe that if we allow hope to germinate and grow inside of us we will see the future of our marriages turn around and see them stand the test of time. Paul shares with us in Corinthians that, *"Love suffers long and is kind; love does not envy; love does not parade itself, is not puffed up; does not behave rudely, does not seek its own, is not provoked, thinks no evil; does not rejoice in iniquity, but rejoices in the truth; bears all things, believes all things,* **hopes all things**, *endures all things."* 1 Corinthians 13:4-7

I believe hope empowers us to keep moving on, believing for God's best for us, fighting for our marriages and families.

The best illustration that comes to mind for me is seeing hope to be like a pilot light. A pilot light is a small gas flame which is kept alight in order to serve as an ignition source for a far more powerful gas element. If the pilot light is extinguished, the entire system dependent on its flame will be shut down. The operation of the gas element will be of no effect.

Hope is our pilot light. It gives us the ability to face the future and to pursue our dreams even if circumstances say differently. When we allow hope to die, so does our dreams and pursuits, not only for ourselves but for our family and our future generations. Let us allow hope to strengthen and empower us today. It will not only strengthen you but also those around you who are looking for signs of hope in today's generation.

3. GOALS

"Then the Lord answered me and said: "Write the vision and make it plain on tablets, that he may run who reads it. For the vision is yet for an appointed time; but at the end it will speak, and it will not lie.

Though it tarries, wait for it; because it will surely come, It will not tarry." Habakkuk 2:2-3

I haven't always been very good at setting goals for my life. I have depended on my husband to make good choices for our family and even for myself. I began to realize that I was becoming lazy concerning my own life. Setting goals is a process that takes every member of the family's input.

If I don't set goals for myself then my family is affected. They will not be encouraged to push forward and set goals for themselves if they see that I am stagnant in my own pursuits. If I am to be "future oriented" I need to set goals for myself with my family in mind.

My husband is a great goal setter and it is very hard for me to keep up to him at times. He oozes with ideas and dreams that seem to seep out of him at every opportunity. I see that as a strength in his life and do not want to hinder the creativity that is so much a part of him. I have learned to support him in this area but it hasn't always been easy. I continually get pushed out of my comfort zone in order to walk alongside of him in these ventures. Do I like change? No, I will be honest with you. I am resistant to change most of the times. I still have to fight against the wall I put up at the first hint of change coming my way. I recognize my behavior and have to tell myself to think it through, give it a chance and don't crush his dreams.

I have seen many relationships struggling because the goals or dreams of one has been crushed or trampled upon by the other partner. We haven't given our spouse the chance to reach their goals or dreams for the future. We take it upon ourselves to resist change and plod on in our everyday life's journey. We snuff out the spirit of adventure and pursuit so life becomes stagnant and uneventful. We are afraid to take chances and see our goals and our spouse's become reality before our eyes. We tell ourselves that it can't be done, it's too risky, and it is out of our comfort zone.

I can mention just a few ventures we have entered in the years we have been married. We have gone from students to missionaries, pastors, students again, evangelist, business owner, bible school teacher to bible school administrator and president to student again to counselor to most recently mental health counselors. Not to forget raising seven wonderful children in the midst of these ventures. These are just a few of the major career and dream makers in these 20 odd years together. Life truly is a journey; you cannot predict each pathway it will branch out to.

I can't tell you that every single dream and every goal that I have supported my husband in has succeeded. I can tell you though that his love and respect for me grows stronger every time I place my trust in him and allow him to follow his dreams. I make his dreams my own and merge my own dreams with his. It becomes something very beautiful and powerful. Others take notice and see the strength in our relationship. It is work, hard work, uncomfortable at times, inconvenient most times but the end results are glorious. *"But you, be strong and do not let your hands be weak, for your work shall be rewarded!"* 2 Chronicles 15:7

We need to learn to appreciate one another along with the dreams and goals that are present. The scripture tell us to be strong and continue to work. Don't let our hands become weak. We will work hard when we have something to accomplish, something to achieve, a goal to meet. The best part of this scripture is the promise that we will be rewarded. It is a promise.

When you look at the dictionary meaning of goals you will understand why we need to work hard in order to see results. The dictionary tells us that goals are "the result or achievement toward <u>which</u> effort is directed; aim; end." [4] It takes effort, work, and hard work in order for us to achieve a desired end.

As a family we had been discussing the possibility of my husband changing jobs in order to receive a permanent 9-5 job. A few years ago he took a position closer to home with a pay cut so he would not have to travel so much. He continued working 12 hour shifts as well and taking on extra jobs in order to supplement the lower pay. It worked for a season but as our family dynamics were changing we realized it would be more beneficial to have a 9-5 job with better pay and more time spent at home.

We began to pray as a family. We also decided to fast individually on different days concerning this. The goal in front of us was the new job. My husband started job searching and sending out resumes. He continued to work at his other jobs with the same zeal and passion. A psychiatrist noticed his passion and work ethic and made recommendations, advising him that day to visit the director of the hospital. When he approached her that same day she said, "Funny you would come in at this time, we just posted a job position today that is 8:30 am - 4:30pm".

To make a long story short, he submitted his resume, received an interview a week later and in another seven days was offered the job. It paid enough to eliminate the other part-time jobs.

Needless to say we are rejoicing in God's provision and the reaching of our goal.

Understanding the process of seeing a goal fulfilled is important.

- *Begin by meeting as a family or couple to discuss future plans/desires/dreams*

- *Write down your goals or vision*

- *Cover them with prayer*

- *Set aside time to fast*

- *Don't allow doubt to cloud your focus*

- *Speak with faith and conviction*

- *Be progressive and work to the best of your ability to see your dreams fullfilled*

- *Have the right attitude. Listen to what God is saying; it's not just about what we want.*

- *Be patient; God's timing is perfect*

In the process of seeing a goal fulfilled we may find ourselves in places that we never planned on being. We may experience a job or career change that we don't quite understand. That is why having a positive attitude and a teachable spirit is so important. In the midst of change we can benefit by growing in God's grace. We can also see more of our character form and gain new skills we never knew we could gain. That position or job may just be our training ground for our future goals.

Bible school was my training ground for some of my future goals even though I did not know it at the time. I was teaching part-time while my husband ran the school and I would help out the best I could. Gradually he began to give me new jobs that stretched me, jobs I was not comfortable in. Book-keeping was one of them. I dislike everything about finances and still do but I began to work on my attitude and learned new skills on the computer. I learned how to deal with conflict and resolution with students as I was gradually being put in charge of the school because of my husband's work schedule. It was a difficult time for me but it pushed me to depend on God and grow in His grace daily.

It reminds me of a story in the Bible of a man called Abraham. Abraham was promised by God that he would have an heir. God took him outside and told him to look towards heaven and count the stars asking if he was able to number them. He then said to him, "So shall your descendants be." The story goes on to tell us that Abraham believed God and it was accounted to him for righteousness.

Abraham did not see the result of that promise or even a hint of its coming fulfillment for a very long time. He had to wait in faith to see the promises of God come to pass. Not only did he have to wait, he had to believe that in his old age he could still father a child. When Isaac finally arrived on the scene Abraham was asked to offer him up a sacrifice to the Lord. Again Abraham had to trust in the promises of God that he would be a father of many nations, even if it meant giving up his only son.

I am sure that Abraham did not expect or plan for the direction that his life took after receiving his promise from God. If you were told that your descendants would be as numerous as the stars I am sure you would be expecting to have children before long. Abraham had to put his focus on God and his promise despite what was happening around him. That is why today he is known as the "father of faith".

I set a goal for finishing this book. You would not believe the distractions and circumstances that kept coming up to deter me away from writing. One recent incident happened early one morning while everyone was asleep. I like to write when the house is quiet and there are not many such times to find especially with seven children in the home. I made myself a cup of coffee, put it on the couch arm and a few seconds later it spilled on me, the couch and eventually the lab top I was writing on. I immediately jumped up, (yes it was hot as well) and dried off the laptop telling myself it is only a few drops. I quickly saved the page I was working on and then the computer went blank! I cannot describe the feeling I had at that moment when I realized that the computer my husband and purchased for me just a few short months ago may be ruined.

I began to pray, petitioning God while running upstairs to tell my husband. He told me to dry it with a hair dryer so I immediately began to do so. While drying the computer board I was fighting the tears. I was very upset with myself for doing something so stupid. It still would not turn on so again I asked advice from my very wise and surprisingly calm husband on what to do next. He simply said, "Try plugging it in and maybe the heat from charging it will dry off the inside." In the meantime he started the process of calling the company we bought the computer from. While doing so we realized that I had not registered the warranty for the computer as yet. I had failed to see the card in the box which had to be emailed or sent in shortly after it was bought to receive the warranty. I was really feeling it now; what was I going to do?

About a half an hour later the unexpected and miraculous happened. I pushed the power button like I had down many times previously but this time the computer came on. I went to all my programs, opened them up and nothing was lost. I was ecstatic. What a wonderful God we serve; despite my foolishness He intervened.

Through this experience I learned that I had not registered my warranty. If I had not spilled the coffee and had this incident I would have never known. This is just is one example of how there are times when we do not understand why we are put in that place or why we have to go through a dry season. We need to realize that in each circumstance, in every situation we can benefit one way or another if we look at it with the eyes of faith. I benefitted by being given the opportunity to register my warranty even though I had forgotten when I first purchased the computer. I also got to experience the wonderful way God can intervene on my behalf to restore and retrieve my book. What an awesome God we serve, who cares personally for us in every situation.

Don't allow the future to lead you where it may. Make choices that benefit yourself and your family. Know that God has plans for you, plans that will give you a future and a hope. Let hope be that pilot light inside of you, burning bright throughout your life's journey, allowing you to push ahead with your dreams. Write down your goals and dreams, cover them with prayer and stand in faith to see them be accomplished. Can this be done? Yes, a thousand times yes, because God is on our side and He cares for the family, the future of our family.

Points to Ponder:

- *Have you had to make choices for your family against the norm of today's society? How have others on the outside reacted to your choices? How has this affected your family?*

- *How has hope brought you further in achieving your goals? Think of some instances in your walk where you only had hope that you would move ahead.*

- *I encourage you to think of some goals you want to accomplish for yourself and your family. Write them down and post them somewhere visible.*

- *Understanding the process of seeing a goal fulfilled is important. What are some things you can do to see your goals fulfilled?*

- *Remember, when you are walking in the very deep waters of life and the tip of your finger is barely peeking out above the water, don't despair; there is still HOPE!*

14 GENERATIONAL BLESSING

"I will bless those who bless you, and I will curse those who curse you; and in you all the families of the earth shall be blessed." Genesis 12:3

We have been taught that generational curses will follow us if we do not acknowledge them and break the power they have over our lives in order for our generation and the next to be free. This is very true and we need to examine our lives and that of our parents to move ahead in our future goals as a family. We can have freedom from the curses of many previous generations. On the other hand, we often fail to acknowledge that blessings are generational as well.

When God was making his covenant with Abraham He was also thinking of us. We too can take hold of the blessing that Abraham received so long ago. How is that possible you may ask? The Apostle Paul answers that question for us. *"If you belong to Christ, then you are Abraham's seed, and heirs according to the promise."* Galatians 3:29

The promise of blessing is for ALL! God promised this blessing to Abraham and his descendants so we are also entitled to these blessings.

God said something very interesting a few chapters later after giving the promise to Abraham. He said, "Should I hide from Abraham what I am doing?" God knew that the blessing that He would pour upon Abraham would be visible to all the nations around him. Let's read this verse together. *"And the Lord said, "Shall I hide from Abraham what I am doing, since Abraham shall surely become a great and mighty nation, and all the nations of the earth shall be blessed in him? For I have known him, in order that he may command his children and his household after him, that they keep the way of the Lord, to do righteousness and justice, that the Lord may bring to Abraham what He has spoken to Him."* Genesis 18:17-19

God promised the blessing but Abraham had to teach and train his children in the ways of the Lord. When Abraham's children would learn to walk in God's ways and grow in Him, God would in turn bring the promise of blessing to the next generation. The blessing of God will grow as we teach and instruct our children. Abraham had to do his part in order to see the blessing promised to him fulfilled. What part are we committing to in order to see the blessing of God poured out upon our children? We need to remember that the greater the commitment, the greater the blessing we will receive for our family.

What are some generational blessings we can commit to or pass down you may ask? I would like to list a few of the many blessings we can bestow on our family, our next generation.

- *A Godly heritage*

- *Prayer*

- *Integrity*

- *Obedience to God's Word*

- *Financial wisdom and security*

- *Healthy living*

- *Strong moral values*

- *Leadership skills*

- *Vibrant and Godly Family traditions*

- *Peace*

- *Forgiveness*

- *Encouraging others*

- *Fruit of the Spirit*

- *Holiness*

- *Christian Ethics*

- *Building relationships*
- *Spiritual community (church family)*

God also promises His Spirit as a blessing to us and our descendants as well. Isaiah prophesied this even before the Holy Spirit was filling the hearts of His people after Pentecost. *"For I will pour water on him who is thirsty, and floods on the dry ground; I will pour My Spirit on your descendants, and My blessing on your offspring."* Isaiah 44:3

The Apostle Peter also spoke of the blessing of the Holy Spirit after being filled and confirmed that it was for us and our children. *"For the promise is to you and to your children and to all who are afar off, as many as the Lord our God will call."* Acts 2:39

This promise is powerful enough not only for our children but for all the generations that would follow us. This blessing would impact all the nations of the earth. Peter quoted from the words of the prophet Joel that it would come to pass that God would pour out His Spirit upon all flesh (Acts 2:16,17).

Do you want the Spirit of God to be present and infilling your children and your children's children? It is possible. In fact it is more than possible, it is promised by God!

BLESSED IS THE MAN.....

"Blessed is the man who fears the Lord, who delights greatly in His commandments. His descendants will be mighty on earth; the generation of the upright will be blessed." Psalm 112:1&2

As a parent we should want our children to experience and have more than we were able to have. We want to see them make a difference in the world, for themselves and for others. We work hard to see this happen, providing food and shelter, education and training. But the most important thing we can do for our children is to fear God and delight in His commandments. *"The fear of the Lord is the beginning of wisdom; a good understanding have all those who do His commandments. His praise endures forever."* Psalm 111:10

When we fear the Lord we have a reverence for God. We will have a great respect for His law and His will. Deep inside will reside the fear of offending him. This fear will in turn lead us to do right, to make the right choices for our children. The fear of the Lord is the origin, the foundation on which wisdom begins. When we fear the Lord we know we cannot go wrong because we have made the right choice. *"Their descendants shall be known among the Gentiles, and their offspring among the people. All who see them shall acknowledge them, that they are the posterity whom the Lord has blessed."* Isaiah 61:9

While doing some research on godly and generational blessing I came upon this wonderful man of God named Jonathan Edwards. He was a puritan preacher from the 1700's and he and his wife Sarah had 11 children. He was well known for the godly values he instilled in each of his children. It was interesting to read this study and see a comparison to his descendant, an ungodly man and his generation that followed. I included the article as follows:

"At the turn of the 20th century, American educator and pastor A.E. Winship decided to trace out the descendants of Jonathan Edwards almost 150 years after his death. His findings are astounding, especially when compared to a man known as Max Jukes. Jukes' legacy came to the forefront when the family trees of 42 different men in the New York prison system traced back to him.

Jonathan Edwards' godly legacy includes:

1 U.S. Vice-President

3 U.S. Senators

3 governors

3 mayors

13 college presidents

30 judges

65 professor,

80 public office holders

100 lawyers and

100 missionaries

Max Jukes' descendants included:

7 murderers

60 thieves

50 women of debauchery

130 other convicts

310 paupers (with over 2,300 years lived in poorhouses)

400 who were physically wrecked by indulgent living

It was estimated that Max Juke's descendants cost the state more than $1,250,000. This is a powerful example showing how a parent's leadership can have a profound effect on their children." [8]

In every family/generation there needs to be someone to start the ball rolling, someone who will take a stand for righteousness and truth, and someone to set the standard for future generations. If your family tree is weak and compromised don't give up, don't throw in the towel because there is still hope. You have the ability to be a trailblazer, someone who can blaze a new trail, a new pathway for the future generation.

We need to realize that the blessing of the Lord is more powerful than the curse. When we set our course to blaze a new trail the curse of generational sin will be no match for the power of the blessing of Christ Jesus through His shed blood. We need to be confident in the power of God's blessing as we walk according to His ways.

Jesus laid his hands on the children that were brought to him and blessed them. The disciples tried to stand in the way of those that wanted their children to be touched by Jesus. However, Jesus told them to let the children come. *"Assuredly, I say to you, whoever does not receive the kingdom of God as a little child will by no means enter it. And He took them up in His arms, laid His hands on them, and blessed them."* Mark 10:15-16

Our children are no different today as they were in Jesus's day. The blessing of the Lord upon children is for our family. We are responsible to bring our children to Jesus through prayer and ask for His blessing to be upon them, that His blessings would flow down upon them, all His promises of blessing. This can only come by walking in His ways and teaching them to our children. As we continue to walk in the blessing of God, the Holy Spirit will work through us and enable us to pass the blessing on to the next generation.

Only a life of total dedication to the Lord can become a channel of blessing to impact the next generation. Refuse to succumb to the world and its love of pleasure and compromise. Lay hold of His promises; lift your children up in prayer, praying in faith for God's blessing to rest upon them. Remind God of His Word and recite His promises out loud, confessing with your mouth to bring about the blessings. As we do this God's promises will be fulfilled. When God promises something we can be assured that it will come to pass.

BLESS THIS HOUSE...

"The Lord has been mindful of us; He will bless us; He will bless the house of Israel; He will bless the house of Aaron. He will bless those who fear the Lord, great and small. May the Lord give you increase more and more; you and your children. May you be blessed by the Lord, who made heaven and earth." Psalm 115:12-15

Everywhere we go we see beautifully designed plaques, picture frames and posters of this statement, "Bless this House." It is hung over our doorways, like a banner proclaiming God's blessing upon our home. Some may not even understand the great significance of this blessing.

God is mindful of us and He will bless us. He will bless those that fear the Lord, great and small. I love dwelling on the fact that God is mindful of us. We are on His mind at all times; we are not forgotten. If we feel that everyone has deserted us, disappointed us or abandoned us we are mistaken because God has never left us. He is mindful of us, our mistakes, our disappointments and or struggles. Despite all of these things He is still by our side, thinking of us and promising to bless us and our family if we fear Him.

"Just as much as the curses will pass down the generation of the wicked so will the blessings of God flow down the generation of the just. *"The curse of the Lord is on the house of the wicked, But He blesses the home of the just."* Proverbs 3:33.

Our home can be a refuge, a place of blessing that even those that enter can benefit from the blessing that is there. Our homes can be the place of contact for those needing a touch from God. If God's blessing resides in our home, it can also touch those who enter. I believe that His blessing is given not just for our home and our children but so that we can share and encourage others with it.

POINTS TO PONDER:

- *How have you seen God's Word work for your family and loved ones? Share a testimony with a friend or neighbour concerning the blessing of God over your life.*

- *In this chapter I have used a lot of scripture to ensure that you understand your part in receiving and imparting the blessings of God to your future generation, your family. I have written them down as a prayer for you. Post it on your fridge and get these scriptures in your spirit by praying this prayer for your family.*

MY GENERATIONAL
BLESSING PRAYER

The fear of the Lord is the beginning of wisdom and as I follow your commandments and precepts I will have good understanding. Blessed am I when I fear you Lord and greatly delight in your commandments. My descendants will be mighty on the earth and my generations will be blessed as I live an upright life. As I live righteously and in integrity my children will be blessed after me. God, you assure me that I belong to You and I am Your child. You will give me and my family one heart and one way so that we may fear Your name forever. This is for the good of my children and their children after them.

God, your mercy is upon me as I fear You and will be upon my generation to future generations. You promise to pour water upon me as I thirst and will flood my dry grounds. Your spirit will be poured out on my descendants and your blessing will be upon my offspring, for your promise is to me and my children and to all others who call upon your name.

You assure me that you will bless those that bless me and curse those that curse me, and your blessing will extend so that other families will be blessed through your promise to me. You have established a covenant between me and You and my descendants after me. It is an everlasting covenant!!! You will be a God to me and my descendants following me. I love your promises.

When Abraham was told he would become a great and mighty nation and all the nations would be blessed in him, he was told in order that he may command his children and his household to keep the way of the Lord. You have affirmed to me in your Word that if I belong to Christ then I am Abraham's seed and I am an heir to the promise, to the same promise you gave Abraham so many years ago. If I raise my children in your ways and precepts to do righteousness and justice you will bring to me as you did Abraham, the promises that were spoken to him. The promise that in my seed all the nations of the earth shall be blessed because I have listened and obeyed Your voice Oh my God.

My descendants will be known throughout the nations. When the world sees them they will acknowledge that they are a people that are blessed. Your Word also tells me that your curse is upon the house of the wicked but upon the home of the just, my home, your blessing resides. Thank you for your blessing upon my family!

You are mindful of me and you will bless me just like you blessed the house of Israel. All those that fear you, despite their size, race or culture, will be blessed as you have blessed even the house of Aaron. Oh my Lord, My God, give me increase more and more, not only for me but for my children. You have made the heaven and the earth yet see me as an individual to be blessed by Your hand.

I will live in prosperity and my children shall inherit the earth, inheriting the promises of God of long life and experiencing the good things of this earth.

This is your Word and this is my prayer. Amen!

(Psalm 111:10, Psalm 112:1,2, Proverbs 20:7, Jeremiah 32:38,39, Luke 1:50, Isaiah 44:3, Acts 2:39, Genesis 12:3, Genesis 17:7, Genesis 18:17-19, Genesis 22:18, Galatians 3:29, Isaiah 61:9, Proverbs 3:33, Psalm 115:12-15, Psalm 25:13)

Notes

1. *Graham, R. (2013) Ruth Bell Graham Quotes. Good Reads.*
   Retrieved from http://www.goodreads.com/quotes/101348-it-is-a-foolish-woman-who-expects-her-husband-to

2. *Central Michigan Life. (2008) People are now waiting longer to get married.*
   Retrieved from http://www.cmlife.com/2008/01/23/peoplearenowwaitinglongertogetmarried/

3. *Hess, A. (2012). The Health Benefits Of Marriage. Focus On The Family Findings.*
   Retrieved from http://www.focusonthefamily.com/about_us/focusfindings/marriage/health-benefits-of-marriage.aspx

4. *Dictionary.com. (2013)*
   Retrieved from http://dictionary.reference.com

5. *Gaines, A. (2010). Benny Hinn Admits 'Friendship' With Paula White But Tells TV Audience It's Over. Charisma Magazine.*

Retrieved from http://www.charismamag.com/site-archives/570-news/featured-news/11683benny-hinn-admits-friendship-with-paula-white-but-tells-tv-audience-its-over

6. *Unifem (2003) Not a minute more: Ending Violence Against Women. United Nations Development Fund for Women. New York.*
Retrieved from http://www.un.org/en/women/endviolence/pdf/VAW.pdf

7. *Spurgeon, C. (1993) Faith's Checkbook.*
Retrieved on http://graceebooks.com/library/Charles%20Spurgeon/CHS_Faiths%20Checkbook.PDF

8. *Edward, J. (2012) Jonathan Edwards Powerful Example of Leaving a Godly Legacy.*
Retrieved on www.unlockingthebible.org/jonathan-edwards-leaving-a

Printed in Canada